PRESS ON
REGARDLESS

PURSUING WHOLENESS AFTER BROKENNESS

GARY TAYLOR

© 2023 Gary Taylor
PRESS ON REGARDLESS

All rights reserved. No part of this publication may be reproduced, stored in a retrieval system, or transmitted in any form or by any means, electronic, mechanical, photocopying, recording, or otherwise without the prior permission of the publisher or in accordance with the provisions of the Copyright, Designs and Patents Act 1988 or under the terms of any license permitting limited copying issued by the Copyright Licensing Agency.

Scripture quotations taken from The Authorized King James Version (KJV). Rights in the Authorized Version in the United Kingdom are vested in the Crown. Reproduced by permission of the Crown's patentee, Cambridge University Press.

Scripture quotations taken from the New King James Version (NKJV)®. Copyright © 1982 by Thomas Nelson. Used by permission. All rights reserved.

Scripture quotations taken from THE MESSAGE (MSG), copyright © 1993, 2002, 2018 by Eugene H. Peterson. Used by permission of NavPress. All rights reserved. Represented by Tyndale House Publishers, a Division of Tyndale House Ministries.

Scripture quotations taken from the Holy Bible, New Living Translation (NLT), copyright ©1996, 2004, 2015 by Tyndale House Foundation. Used by permission of Tyndale House Publishers, Inc., Carol Stream, Illinois 60188. All rights reserved.

Scripture quotations taken from the Holy Bible, New International Version®, (NIV®). Copyright ©1973, 1978, 1984, 2011 by Biblica, Inc.™ Used by permission of Zondervan. All rights reserved worldwide.

Scripture quotations taken from the (NASB®) New American Standard Bible®, Copyright © 1960, 1971, 1977, 1995, 2020 by The Lockman Foundation. Used by permission. All rights reserved. lockman.org.

Library of Congress Control Number: 2023921976

ISBN: 979-8-218-32147-5

Published by:
Resurgence Publishing, LLC
P.O. Box 514
Goshen, OH 45122
www.resurgencebooks.org

Cover Design: Aaftab Sheikh

Printed in the United States of America

DEDICATION

Press On Regardless is dedicated to anyone who has been broken in life or wounded in ministry. This book was written to be a source of hope, and encouragement to never give up believing God will bring you to a better, brighter day.

> "I would have lost heart, unless I had believed
> that I would see the goodness of the Lord
> In the land of the living."
> Psalm 27:13 (NKJV)

RECOMMENDATIONS

"Every time Gary Taylor has filled the pulpit for me at Restoration Church, he has blessed our congregation with a fresh word of hope and encouragement. Now, with the release of his book, 'Press On Regardless,' he brings that same message in written form to inspire and impact a much larger audience. Gary writes with candor and conviction about his own struggles of being broken and crushed in the crucible of life, and points us to biblical examples of the same, while at the same time refusing the temptation to languish in despair or resign to defeat. Instead, he continually points with assurance to a better day and a brighter promise for those who keep their trust in God and refuse to quit. His words ring with the authenticity that can only come from someone who has held onto God and experienced the grace of God holding onto him."

- John V. Morgan, Lead Pastor,
Restoration Church, Jacksonville, FL

"Gary Taylor is no stranger to the fact none of us are immune to the perils of life in a broken world. He is equally acquainted with the truth that no broken life escapes the care and provision of God, if one is willing to Press On, Regardless. This story, his story, will provide a roadmap for anyone struggling with the pain of unexpected tragedy and heartache and will point to the healing which God will bring through the journey toward Him. If you are grappling with the pain of disappointment in life, this book is for you!"

- Toby Morgan, Administrative Bishop,
Virginia Church of God State Executive Offices

"In one discourse, Gary has opened his Heart, shown us of God's Help, and gives the reader immense Hope! Wisdom and Life Application from years of Pastoral ministry and the 'walking out' of his own faith, lends great authenticity to this work. A guide grounded in Scriptures, here, you will find a path to renewed Spiritual, Relational and Emotional Health as well as Wholeness in the aftermath of life's trauma and tragedy."

- Jon Quigley, Lead Pastor,
Community Worship Center, Riverview, Florida

"Press On Regardless: Get it, read it, and pray as you walk with him in his storm. In this book, he shares the story of his heartache and his healing. I believe, in its pages you will discover that God really does work all things together for our good."

- Freddie Edwards, Lead Pastor,
The Sanctuary, Sylacauga, Alabama

"Press On Regardless: Pursuing Wholeness After Brokenness is a 'must read' for all who face a dark night of the soul. In it, we learn that no distance is too great for Jesus to overcome, and no heart is too broken for Jesus to heal. There is hope! Sorrow can be turned into joy!"

- Mark L. Williams, D.Min, D.D., Lead Pastor,
North Cleveland Church of God, Cleveland, TN

"Gary Taylor, besides being an incredible friend, preacher, and Christian, is now an author! This body of work will captivate you from the introduction with its conversational truths. You will find this raw, real, and relatable, but more importantly, you'll discover a bright light of hope that may have been dimmed by life's speed bumps, road blocks, or major accidents. I highly recommend this book for anyone, no matter how fresh or vintage their wounds and scars. I believe this book will be a giant step forward in getting past the past!"

- Patrick Casey, Lead Pastor,
Rise Church, Mobile AL

"In writing 'Press On Regardless,' Gary Taylor vividly relives his very real and very personal trauma. But what's more, he offers his readers personal proof of Paul's promise in Galatians 6:9: 'Let us not become weary in doing good, for at the proper time we will reap a harvest if we do not give up.' In these pages, Gary gives comfort for the weary and hope for the brokenhearted. He reminds us that God cares about our troubles and will guide us to safety."

- Bishop Ken Shelton,
Shelton Covenant Ministries

"'Press On Regardless' is written with a convincing trust in God's power to sustain us during life-altering events. Gary Taylor speaks with authenticity and transparency and is an excellent writer. This book will propel the reader to take hold of God's promises and walk into victory!"

- Rhonda Brown, State Director,
Florida Church of God Women's Ministries

"I am so grateful that the Lord put it in Gary's heart to write this inspiring book that helps to restore hope and healing for anyone who has experienced brokenness in their life. Using both scripture and personal experience, Gary takes us on a journey that begins with pain, continues through perseverance, but ends with praise. Jamie and I believe so much in the message of this book that we have made it required reading for every person going through addiction recovery at City of Lights Dream Center."

- Victor Massey, Lead Pastor,
Cooper City Church of God, Cooper City, Florida

"My dear friend Gary Taylor has written a must-read book for any broken soul who is searching for the road that leads to recovery from life's hurts and setbacks. It is a veritable roadmap that will point the way back to wholeness."

- Tommy Quick, Lead Pastor,
Dogwood Hills Church, Brewton, Alabama

"Press On Regardless" not only captivates the reader with its profound insights but also serves as a guiding light through the tumultuous journey of life. Each chapter is a testimony to Gary Taylor's deep understanding of the human spirit and its incredible capacity for growth and healing. It is a masterful blend of personal anecdotes, spiritual truth, and practical advice—a must-read for anyone seeking guidance, healing, or simply a reminder of the strength that lies within us all."

- Dr. Devin Stephenson, President,
Northwest Florida State College, Niceville, Florida

"Press On Regardless" is a captivating read that truly opened my eyes to the power of forgiveness and new beginnings. The author's presentation of facts and personal anecdotes from God's Word shed light on the transformative nature of letting go, accepting what you can't change, and embracing grace. The book celebrates the process of recovery, reminding us that it's a journey worthy of celebration. It's a heartwarming and soul-nourishing read, akin to honey for the soul, emphasizing the importance of pressing on despite life's challenges. "Never quit, press on regardless" is the resounding message that resonates throughout this inspirational book, making it a must-read for anyone seeking personal growth and healing.

- Janet Swanson, Worship Leader,
Growth Church, Naples, FL

CONTENTS

FOREWORD 11

INTRODUCTION 12

CHAPTER 1: Life-Altering 18

CHAPTER 2: Shaken Faith 30

CHAPTER 3: Life Is Not Always Fair 48

CHAPTER 4: Rejection Hurts 58

CHAPTER 5: Telling Anger Goodbye 70

CHAPTER 6: Facts About Forgiveness 80

CHAPTER 7: The Road To Recovery 100

CHAPTER 8: Overcoming Offenses 114

CHAPTER 9: Mastering Mistakes 126

CHAPTER 10: Breaking Influences 132

CHAPTER 11: Peace With Your Past 144

CHAPTER 12: The Scarred Life 156

CHAPTER 13: God's Affirmation 166

CHAPTER 14: Extreme Makeover 180

CHAPTER 15: Never Quit! 188

ABOUT THE AUTHOR 198

FOREWORD

I have known Gary Taylor longer than either of us would like to admit. We first met as students at Lee College in the seventies and have maintained a healthy and hilarious friendship over the decades. I was very glad to hear Gary was writing a book, and I was not disappointed by the honesty and candor he shared.

There are three things I appreciate about this book specifically. First, I appreciate that this book is scriptural. Historically, I doubt there's ever been a time when we have needed more of the compass of scripture. Every page of this book is filled with sound biblical principles, stories, and quotes.

Second, I appreciate the powerful illustrations and narratives that educate and inspire. Third, I greatly appreciate the transparency of Gary's very personal journey through suffering. If I were to choose a favorite chapter, it would probably be the chapter on the scarred life. That chapter means a lot to me because I remember when Gary went through those devastating valleys. I can't communicate how much I respect how he handled those painful seasons with faithfulness and integrity.

Although this book deals with life's darkest issues, it is very encouraging and hopeful, reflecting Gary's personality as a gifted encourager. I would share this book with anyone going through a difficult time. I can see this book being used as an evangelistic tool. I also think it is a natural resource for small study groups. It is ideal for family devotional time. Since each chapter stands alone, selective chapters are helpful for discussion starters with counseling clients, students, or parishioners.

H. Edward Stone Ph.D.
Lee University
Cleveland, Tennessee

INTRODUCTION

Jesus began His earthly ministry by going into the synagogue (Luke 4:16-20) and announcing His assignment for coming to earth by reading aloud the scripture, Isaiah 61:1-3, "The Spirit of The Lord God is upon me, because The Lord has anointed me to preach good tidings to the poor; He has sent me to heal the brokenhearted, to proclaim liberty to the captives, and the opening of the prison to those who are bound; to proclaim the acceptable year of The Lord, and the day of vengeance of our God; to comfort all who mourn, to console those who mourn in Zion, to give them beauty for ashes, the oil of joy for mourning, the garment of praise for the spirit of heaviness: that they may be called trees of righteousness, the planting of The Lord, that He may be glorified."

In reading this Scripture, Jesus confirmed that emotional healing was a priority in His assignment from the Father. The statements, "He has sent me to heal the brokenhearted" and "to comfort all who mourn," give hope to everyone dealing with emotional brokenness. Hope is essential in recovering from broken hearts and dreams. Throughout His ministry, Jesus offered people hope. He motivated them to believe for more, to face their fears, and to overcome failures.

At the end of Jesus' ministry, He instructed His disciples to "Go into all the world and preach the Good News to everyone, everywhere" (Mark 16:15). Jesus began and finished His earthy ministry by offering hope. The Good News that Jesus spoke of is a message of hope. Hope has to do with expectation. It is the desire for something good to happen in the future. Jesus told His disciples to take His message of hope everywhere because it was for everyone. In other words, don't leave anyone out.

"Leave No Man Behind" has been a creed of the United States military services from its beginning. The creed started with the French and Indian War in 1756 twenty years before the United States declared independence from the British. The interpretation of the phrase included medical treatment for the wounded, the recovery of military members' bodies killed in action, and attempting to rescue prisoners of war. This kind of loyalty to one another is extremely rare and has its risks. Yet, when a soldier is entering combat there are few things more reassuring than to know your military brothers and sisters would go to these measures for you. Jesus began the "Leave No Man Behind" motto in Mark 16:15 with his Good News message of hope being taken to everyone, everywhere.

As Christians, we must continually work to develop a culture of hope to leave no one behind. Dr. Freddie Gage, a great Southern Baptist Evangelist for more than sixty years said, "The Christian army is the only army that shoots and buries its wounded." Unfortunately, there is some truth in Dr. Gage's statement. Every wounded soldier still has value, and restoration ministry needs to be a priority. Pastor Bill Bennot of Journey of Grace Church in Cape Town, South Africa, spoke of this priority when he said, "How we walk with the broken speaks louder than how we sit with the great."

Author Hal Lindsey said, "Man can live about forty days without food, eight days without water, four minutes without air, but not one second without hope." However the wound occurred, no matter the depth of pain experienced, or the destruction that came, there is hope for you. Proverbs 13:12 (NIV) "Hope deferred makes the heart sick, but a longing fulfilled is a tree of life." When hope is lost it makes us sick emotionally. You can see it in a person's face, eyes, and body language. You can hear it in their voice. When people lose hope, it is so easy for them to give up on life. The good news is that hope can be rediscovered. Listen to how Job describes his rediscovery of hope in Job 14:7-9, "If a tree is cut down, there is hope that it will sprout again and grow new branches. Though its roots have grown old in the earth and its stump decays, at the scent of water it may bud and sprout again like a new seedling." Think about an old decaying tree sprouting new branches because of hope! What brought the tree down? Who knows? Here's what we know: whatever brought the tree down could not keep it down because of hope. At the scent of water, it begins to bud again. The scent of water represents hope. Job didn't say at the sight of water, but the scent of water. Just the scent of water is enough to bring hope. Hope isn't always the result of a big event or major happening. It can come from a simple prayer, scripture verse, word of encouragement, book, poem, sermon, or song. Hope meets you where you are, and moves you forward. So keep in mind that whatever brought you down cannot keep you down because of the power of hope. Job told us about an old broken-down stump having the ability to sprout again because of hope. The power of hope gives you the desire to believe again, dream again, and try again.

Hope doesn't mean your world is perfect, or that you never have any problems, anxiety, or stress. Hope is the expectation of a better future that gives you the courage to walk through each stage of emotional recovery on your way to wholeness. The word journey means the act of traveling from one place to another. On your journey from brokenness to wholeness remember the following:

GOD CARES

God cares about everyone who is hurting, whether their suffering is physical, emotional, mental, spiritual, or financial. The Apostle Peter gives some great advice in 1 Peter 5:7, "Cast all your anxiety on God because he cares for you." Peter was a commercial fisherman by trade. The word cast he used means to release. An experienced fisherman knows that to be successful, you must know how to release a net. If not, your catch would be few, if any. Success often depends on knowing how to let go. So much of your prayer life depends on knowing how to release burdens, stress, and frustration to the Lord. The Apostle Peter wrote that we can release it all to God because He cares about us.

In Matthew 6:25-34, Jesus describes God as a caring Father. Jesus referred to God as a parent when he addressed him as our "Heavenly Father" twice in this scripture. He used the illustration that our Heavenly Father provides for birds and flowers as examples of the Father's caring nature. Jesus then reassured His followers by saying that you are far more valuable to the Father than they are. A parent's greatest possession is their children. Our Heavenly Father loves and cares about you because you are His greatest possession!

GOD COMFORTS

II Corinthians 1:3-4 the Apostle Paul describes God as the "Father of compassion and the God of all comfort, who comforts us in all our troubles." Paul reassures us that God doesn't abandon us in hard times but sticks with us, comforting us in our difficulties and disappointments.

God comforts us through his presence. Paul knew about the powerful presence of the Lord. He wrote in 2 Timothy 4:10-17 about being deserted by Demas, abandoned by Crescent, forsaken by Titus, and terribly wounded by Alexander. Yet, while alone and hurting Paul stated in verse 17, "But the Lord stood with me, and gave me strength." What an awesome testimony of the Lord's presence! When you are alone and hurting the Lord stands with you. His presence always gives us strength and comfort.

GOD COMPLETES

According to Colossians 2:10, "You are complete in him (Christ)." No matter how broken or hurt you are, God can heal you. You don't have to live wounded for the rest of your life. David wrote in Psalm 147:3, "He heals the brokenhearted, binding up their wounds." God loves to rebuild, repair, and restore people.

Hebrews 12:2 identifies Jesus as the "author and finisher" of our faith. Whatever Jesus begins, He finishes, even if the material He is working with isn't perfect. Our flaws, imperfections, weaknesses, limitations, failures, and struggles will not keep God from restoring us because He works with us with completion in mind. He already sees the finished product!

Your future will not be identical to your past. There will be challenges and changes, and it won't always be easy. But, can you do it? Yes, you can, and it will be worth it. As you walk through each stage of recovery, you become stronger because God is completing you. He is working "all things together" for your good, according to Romans 8:28. Nothing that has happened to you will stop God from finishing what He started in you. We see this in the life of Joseph. After what his brothers had done to him, and after the years of separation, Joseph confidently told them, "God turned into good what you meant for evil" (Genesis 50:20). The good that came out of Joseph's story, was intended by God to be a blessing for him, his father, and his brothers. After his brother's rejection, betrayal, and deception, God cared for, comforted, and completed Joseph. Then, to top it off, He positioned Joseph to lead Egypt through a famine. God will not leave you wounded but will restore and complete you so that He can position you to be effective for his Kingdom.

Gary Taylor

CHAPTER 1

LIFE-ALTERING

Life-altering events are part of everyone's journey. As we go through life, change is inevitable. We anticipate many of these events and prepare for things such as graduations, weddings, anniversaries, the birth of babies, new careers, new homes, promotions, and retirements, to name a few. These important milestones enrich our lives with a sense of accomplishment and fulfillment. We celebrate them because they are giant steps forward as we pursue our life's journey.

However, there are times when life is interrupted by unexpected and tragic crises. It might be an automobile accident that took a family member or friend. Or perhaps a heart attack that prematurely ended the life of a loved one. Maybe it was a terminal cancer diagnosis that gave no hope. Or, sadly, a baby that was born with a handicap or disability. We often hear about women raped, children who are abused or trafficked, and the all-too-often school shootings. Then there are divorces, the betrayal of a friend, bankruptcy, or the lost job. We are overwhelmed with information these days, and it is common to hear about natural disasters caused by hurricanes, tornados, or earthquakes. The list goes on and on.

When painful, life-altering events happen, we are often left broken and devastated. They force us to cross thresholds that can change our lives forever and take us into unfamiliar territory. No amount of time, prayer, or counseling can fully prepare a person for this sort of devastation when it happens. Perhaps one or more of these painful events has happened to you. Suddenly, you felt the disappointment of what happened and the reality that your life may never be the same. Fear of the unknown and the challenge of continuing with life left you in disbelief. Overwhelmed, you had far more questions than answers, and the questions kept coming. How could God have allowed it? Why did this happen? How do I process it? Where do I go from here? What does my future hold? What good could ever come out of it? The one thing that adverse life-altering events have in common is loss. Someone or something of great value is lost. There is a short book in the Old Testament named after Ruth, its primary character. It tells the story of a woman named Naomi who suffered an enormous loss. Because of famine, Naomi, her husband Elimelech, and their two sons left their home in Bethlehem and moved to Moab with the hopes of beginning a new life for their family. After relocating and settling in Moab, her husband died. Naomi experienced the painful, life-altering experience of losing her husband. As a widow, her world changed. While working through the shock and grief of losing her soulmate, she had to manage all the responsibilities of everyday life as a single mother.

As if that weren't enough, one of Naomi's sons died. Now as a widow, she is faced with perhaps the greatest heartbreak and loss in life, the death of a child. Then the unthinkable happens; her other son also died. In Moab, roughly sixty miles from her home in Bethlehem, Naomi had to face the painful, life-altering loss of her husband and two sons. No doubt, when Elimelech and Naomi relocated to Moab, they did so, hoping it would be a place for new opportunities to advance, prosper, and set their family up for a great future. Instead, it turned out to be a disaster. There are not enough words in one's vocabulary to adequately describe Naomi's loss that left her grieving alone in Moab.

Naomi decided to return home to Bethlehem, which is very common when tragedy strikes. Returning to the familiar often creates a sense of security for those who have experienced incredible loss and are trying to find their way in life. Naomi's daughter-in-law, Ruth, went with her back to Bethlehem, while her daughter-in-law, Orpah, returned to her family in Moab. Upon arriving in Bethlehem, people began recognizing her and asking, "Is that you, Naomi?" Naomi responded, "Don't call me Naomi anymore. Instead, call me Mara." The name Naomi means pleasant, while the name Mara means bitter. Naomi said, "I left Bethlehem full and came home empty. Why has God allowed me to suffer such tragedies?" Her grief was beyond human comprehension. Grieving the loss of her husband represented her past. A past life that had become only a memory. She would never wake up with him again in the morning, prepare him a meal, or share laughter. The past was over. Getting over the past can be a long and painful process. Naomi likely felt like she could never stop mourning the loss of her two sons. Grieving the loss of her sons represented her future. She would never know the joy of grandchildren or be able to babysit, feed, or play with them. The cycle of life had been broken for Naomi. It was too much. There was loss everywhere she looked, the past, present, or future.

That's why she screamed with a broken heart, "I left home full, but I have come home empty!" Life had been so unkind and unfair to Naomi that she told the Bethlehem community, "I'm not pleasant anymore; I'm bitter!" The adverse life-altering events had changed her. Naomi's announcement revealed that she was broken, bitter, angry, and empty. She had lost all control of her life, and her present looked nothing like her past. Naomi was not the same person who left Bethlehem with her husband and two sons, excited about beginning a new life in Moab. Naomi's life had been painfully altered, her loss unimaginable, and she was broken and bitter.

This story reminds me of my own. Within three years (2008-2011), I experienced three harrowing life-altering events. First, my youngest brother, Darren, committed suicide. He was forty-three years of age, married, and had two sons and a grandson. Our family came together in shock and disbelief to weep, mourn, pray, and make funeral arrangements. Pastor John Hewett ministered to our family at Darren's funeral with wisdom and grace. He had counseled Darren on many occasions and shared with us how Darren loved the Lord with all his heart. Then he quoted Romans 10:10, which reminded us that believing with your heart makes you right with God. Pastor Hewett told us that Darren's battles were in his mind and that people could love God in their hearts and have conflicts in their minds.

You can lose a battle but win the war. His message was a great source of strength for our family.

The tragic loss of Darren was unlike anything we had ever been through. It left us confused, asking why, which often goes unanswered. The painful, life-altering event of Darren's death left a massive hole in our hearts.

Then, fifteen months after Darren's death, my dad, Reverend Wayne Taylor, died. He had a history of heart problems. In 2009 he underwent heart surgery and passed away only five weeks later. Dad was my best friend and mentor. In June 1975, I told my parents I had accepted my call into ministry. Dad said, I have known it all your life but never told you because it had to be between you and the Lord. My dad had great success as a pastor and church leader. He wisely coached me about ministry. He taught me to do and be my best and not get caught up in the competition that often exists in contemporary church ministry. He never pressured me to follow his path but always encouraged me to follow what I believed the Lord had for me. He was consistently available for a talk if I needed him. At times, his suggestions weren't what I wanted to hear, but he never failed to offer sound advice. He was my biggest fan! His absence left a big void in my life that no one else could fill.

Then, in 2011, my world fell apart with the loss of my thirty-year marriage. I did everything possible to save it, but it wasn't enough. The death of my marriage left me devastated. It took a toll on every aspect of my life. In addition, my two sons (who were in their twenties) were also dealing with the destruction of our family unit.

A ministry leader whom I highly regarded encouraged me to continue in ministry. So, I continued traveling and ministering in local churches—a decision I later regretted. Now I know I should have taken time out from ministry for healing. I needed restoration. I was so broken and had lost so much weight that I looked sick, and there were rumors that I had cancer. I was hurting so badly that, at times, I couldn't think properly. Yet, I continued in ministry as I was advised. I still believed in the miracle of reconciliation for my marriage. However, the challenges of continuing in church ministry under such heavy circumstances lead me to a deep, dark depression.

In July 2011, I met Marion & Cindy Uter, a great couple from Fort Lauderdale, Florida, and they invited me to their home. I accepted their invitation, and although I barely knew them, I stayed for several weeks. They asked only two things of me. First, I had to eat breakfast with them every morning. Second, I had to eat dinner with them every evening. Every morning and evening, they shared the Word of God with me, telling me God was not finished with me, God's purpose for my life had not been fulfilled yet, and my best days were ahead of me. I was amazed at how God used these new friends to minister to me. Spending time with them in Fort Lauderdale allowed me to relax. But that's not all that was happening. While I was there, God began to restore me to emotional and spiritual health.

One Friday morning, I sat on the back porch, praying for direction. Marion and Cindy's home was on a canal directly across from the Fort Lauderdale Yacht Club. As I prayed, a yacht docked across the water from me. I didn't notice much at first, but when I looked closer, I saw the yacht's name was Press On Regardless. Inwardly I prayed, "Lord, you have spoken to me through a yacht!" I was so excited that I ran to my car and drove to the yacht club. I walked up to the yacht, boarded, and knocked on the door. A distinguished senior gentleman came to the door. I introduced myself and asked if he was the owner. He said he was and introduced himself as Skip Allen, Sr. Then, he graciously invited me in, introduced me to his wife, Helen, and led me to their living quarters. I shared my story and how I believed the Lord spoke to me through the name, Press On Regardless. He was the founder of the magazine Southern Boating. He looked at me with a big smile and said, "I'm so happy the Lord used my yacht to speak to you."

Press On Regardless was now a part of my spirit. I told a group of my prayer partners about the experience. I began to feel refreshed. It was the best I had felt in a long, long time. This was the inspiration, the turnaround I needed. I had received my word from the Lord to Press On Regardless. I just knew the miracle of reconciliation for my marriage was on its way!

Five days later, I was notified that my wife had filed divorce papers. All at once, I felt crushed again. This reality hit me hard. I turned inward and fell into a deep depression that felt like a thick heavy cloud. The spirit of suicide was very present and very real.

The following week, I returned home to visit my mother, Mildred. While staying with her, she could sense my despair. One day she looked straight at me and said, "Don't you do something stupid! I've already lost one son!" I didn't want to add heaviness to my mother with my depression, but she discerned it. She, too, was saddened by my failed marriage, but she always stood by me. Facing those three life-altering events not only affected me, they also affected our entire family.

I was depressed and felt defeated. I couldn't understand why things were turning out like they were when I was praying and standing on God's Word. I went to see my friends, Pastor Toby & Diane Morgan. As we discussed the divorce, the Morgans gave me great advice and counsel. Toby said, "No matter how much you pray, fast, or quote scripture, there will be no reconciliation because there is no agreement." He quoted Amos 3:3, "How can two walk together unless they agree." I didn't want to hear that, but I knew he was right. Reality can be so cruel. It was difficult to accept that my marriage was over when I had fought so long and hard for it. I was forced to make decisions that went against my core values. I knew what had happened was not God's will, yet I had no control over it.

I received news that a judge had set an October court date for the divorce. It felt surreal to think my marriage was dissolving. Oh, how I dreaded that day! As the date approached, I became more and more stressed. The reality of what was happening, and the anxiety I felt, were unlike anything I could have imagined. I had lost over thirty pounds and felt like a dead man as I walked with my attorney into the Fort Worth, Texas County Courthouse that Monday morning, October 24, 2011. Standing before a judge and watching him sign divorce documents that terminated my marriage was excruciating. I couldn't believe what I was witnessing. Thirty years of memories flashed through my mind in minutes. My marriage was gone, and I left the courthouse that day, divorced. I had prayed, fasted, and believed for a miracle in my marriage, and I lost. It was such a traumatic experience that, though I did my best to hide them, the tears continued for weeks. I had never experienced such deep pain. Now I know why Malachi 2:16 says that God hates divorce. It's because of the brokenness and pain that follows. The effects of divorce carry over to so many people, and they last for many years.

The word was out that I was divorced, and everything changed. Many pastors in whose churches I had previously ministered would no longer return my phone calls. Ministry doors were closing. The baggage from the divorce seemed like too much. My marriage was over at age fifty-four, and my world turned upside down. I accepted my call into ministry and preached my first sermon at age 18. Ministry was all I had known my entire adult life. I loved the ministry and connecting with people. The possibility of losing my ministry added to my grief and sorrow. I often wondered if I would also lose what I believed I was born to do. I had fought for my miracle and lost. The disappointment of being where I was at my age and the stage of my life was overwhelming. I should have been experiencing my best and most productive days, but instead, I lost my marriage and possibly my ministry. The weight of the divorce and the shame and embarrassment of what had happened were so heavy that I couldn't see any future ministry.

I was an emotional wreck. The ramifications of the divorce affected every part of my life. I felt like damaged goods and such a failure. Now, who would want me to minister? It seemed like there was darkness everywhere I looked. I was tormented in my mind with thoughts that taunted me, how can you get up and preach to people about miracles, but you didn't get yours? I was at the point of giving up the ministry and finding a secular job. I had come to the end of me. There was nothing left in me. Like Naomi, I was angry, broken, bitter, and empty. The divorce, betrayal, deception, brokenness, depression, and loss were too much. I was done!

Now, let's return to the Book of Ruth where we read about Naomi's loss and bitterness. When Naomi returned home to Bethlehem, she was bitter. But that was not the end of her story. The loss of her husband and sons were painful chapters in her life. However, life is like a book with many chapters. Every chapter in a person's life does not have to be perfect to have a great life. Naomi returned home believing her life was over because of the loss of her husband and sons. Once she was back in Bethlehem, she learned the powerful lesson that God could bring good out of bad. Romans 8:28 doesn't teach us that everything in life is good or that God causes everything, but that, God works all things together for our good. God includes the good, the bad, the ugly, the painful, and the shameful of the past in preparing us for our future. What Naomi lost in Moab would not be her final chapter in life because God was working for her good even when she couldn't believe it, see it, or feel it.

It was harvest season, and Naomi's daughter-in-law, Ruth, went to a field and began picking up the leftover barley so they could bake bread. While Ruth was working, the owner of the barley field, a man named Boaz, noticed her. Soon, Boaz met Ruth, and a love story began. This unlikely couple, Boaz and Ruth, married and had a son they named Obed. Obed fathered Jesse, the grandchild that Naomi had given up on. When Jesse grew up, he fathered eight sons. The youngest was named David. Later, Samuel the prophet anointed David as king over Israel when he was just a young lad tending his father's sheep. The New Testament book of Matthew reveals that twenty-eight generations passed from David to Joseph, the husband of Mary, the mother of Jesus the Messiah. Naomi had no way of knowing that when she was rocking her baby boy Obed to sleep, she was holding the great-grandfather of King David of Israel.

What seemed to be a tragic end to Naomi's hope was an opportunity for God to give her a brand new destiny. One that she could not have even known to hope for. Her return to Bethlehem amid her grief was an act of faith that eventually changed the world! Naomi's story reminds us that there is hope after loss. In the story of Naomi, we learn that good chapters can outweigh the bad and that God works all things for our good.

I was dreading Thanksgiving and the upcoming holidays. This was the third grief-filled holiday season in four years. One day, as I prayed, my mind was filled with questions and doubts about the future. Gently, the Holy Spirit reassured me that my divorce had not released me from my call to ministry I accepted when I was eighteen years old. Then the Holy Spirit reminded me of the words, Press On, Regardless, an affirmation I needed to hear again. I didn't hear those words with natural hearing, but I heard them in my spirit. I remembered the day the yacht bearing those words docked in front of me during my stay in Fort Lauderdale. The memory encouraged me so much that I replayed it repeatedly in my mind. The Holy Spirit used that encouragement to help me settle the issue of my future. I determined that I would continue in ministry and press on, regardless!

LIFE-ALTERING

The following week, my friend Pastor Freddie Edwards called me. As we talked, he told me he had planned a ministry trip to India for December 2011. His wife, Suzette, originally planned to go along, but she had changed her mind. Freddie didn't want to travel alone, so he asked me if I wanted to go with him. I agreed and started making preparation.

The time finally came, and we made the trip to India. On the first Sunday in India, we ministered in multiple services at a conference where the crowds reached eight to ten thousand people. What a blessing to know that during this painful time in my personal life, when I felt so lost and alone at Christmas, God reassured me that He still had confidence in my ministry. There I was, in a part of the world where I had never been, ministering to people I had never met. Freddie Edward's invitation to be part of his ten-day ministry trip was just what I needed, and I prayed for God to use me to minister to the people of India.

Even though 2011 had been a personal disaster, I knew I was blessed to have family, friends, and pastors that never gave up on me. Their prayers, words of support, and encouragement helped me get through the year, but I knew I needed more. So I began professional counseing with a Christian counselor. My counselor coached me to release the past, accept what I could not change, and he helped me move forward in life. I needed to learn these lessons to heal and move on with my life. Counseling is not a quick fix. It can be slow and painful. Sometimes, it hurts to get well.

The year, 2012, turned into an amazing time of ministry for me. It took off so fast that I could hardly keep up the pace. I was beginning to heal and the Lord opened doors for me to minister to forty-nine congregations in eleven states. I saw thousands of worshipers blessed by the Lord. I also witnessed many salvations, miracles, healings, and spiritual breakthroughs. The demanding schedule wasn't easy, but I kept hearing in my spirit the words, press on regardless. It is incredible what God can do through our brokenness.

The following year, there were even more opportunities to reach people for Christ. Sometimes, preachers wear out by keeping a busy schedule. However, I was getting stronger with each passing day. Sunday, May 5, 2013, marked the fifteenth anniversary of City Hope Church, where Jerry and Jerri Taylor, my brother and his wife, were the founding pastors. They had planned an anniversary celebration, and I was excited to be able to attend. During the afternoon church picnic, Jerri introduced me to a lady named Penny Weeks. We talked awhile that afternoon, and I must admit there was an instant attraction. So, I called and invited her to dinner the next night, but she declined. She told me that her husband had died of cancer two years earlier. She told me she had not dated anyone and didn't plan to do so. I didn't want to ignore her feelings, but I knew something about loss, too, so I tried again. Eventually, through our talks and my persistence, Penny finally agreed to have dinner with me. It was set for Friday, May 10, 2013. We had such a great time that night, laughing and talking, that we stayed at the restaurant for over three hours. Fifty-two days later, we were married on July 1, 2013.

Looking back, I believe I had gone as far as I could on the healing journey, by myself. God placed a beautiful, smart, and strong woman in my life to complete my healing. Penny is my helpmate, best friend, and partner in ministry. God brought two people together, who had each experienced devastating, life-altering events, and began new chapters for us. We adopted the motto, The rest of our lives, will be the best of our lives. It pays to press on regardless.

CHAPTER 2
SHAKEN FAITH

The writer of the New Testament book of Hebrews encouraged Christians who encountered opposition, persecution, and suffering not to throw away their faith. Hebrews 10:35 states, "Do not throw away this confident trust in the Lord. Remember the great reward it brings you!" This is wonderful counsel for anyone whose faith has been shaken by a major disappointment in life. Do not throw your faith away, no matter what happens or comes your way.

A broken marriage, a broken heart, and broken dreams can leave your faith shaken, which can cause you to question what you believe. Decisions you were once sure of, you now second guess. Your core value system is addled. The loss of confidence can leave you doubting who you are and uncertain about your future.

We often look at Bible characters as superhuman people who never encountered difficulties. We view them as heroes who always had it together, got it right, and had the correct answer. Yet, throughout the Bible, we find people who dealt with circumstances or situations that shook their faith. So let's look at seven men from the Bible and what caused their faith to be shaken.

ABRAHAM'S FAITH WAS SHAKEN BECAUSE OF IMPATIENCE

In Genesis 12, God called Abraham to become the father of a great nation. This nation would come forth in the future through Abraham's children beginning with a son named Isaac, (Romans 9:7). God promised Abraham that his descendants would be as the sand on the Earth, (Genesis 13:16) and the stars in the sky, (Genesis 15:5); His point being they are both innumerable. So the future looked great for Abraham. The only problem was that his wife Sarah couldn't have children, (Genesis 11:29-30). Now isn't that just like God, to make such a promise and then let you marry a woman who can't have children?

When God made this promise to Abraham, he was seventy-five years old, and Sarah was sixty-five. Ten years later, Abraham and Sarah still had no son. The clock was ticking. Time was against them. Out of impatience, Sarah suggested that Abraham should sleep with her servant, Hagar, thus building a family through her. Due to his impatience, Abraham agreed with the plan. This is evidence that Abraham had not yet arrived at being "fully persuaded" that God could perform his promise, as stated in Romans 4:21. As a result of this arrangement, Hagar became pregnant and gave Abraham a son. During Hagar's pregnancy, the Angel of The Lord appeared and told her to name the baby Ishmael. The angel told Hagar that Ishmael would be as wild as an untamed donkey. It turned out just as the angel said. Ishmael would always be in conflict. Plans and decisions made out of impatience usually end up creating conflict.

Years later, at ninety-nine, Abraham experienced God's presence and entered a covenant relationship with God (Genesis 17). In one year, Sarah gave birth to their promised son, Isaac. God did for Abraham and Sarah in one year what they couldn't do for themselves in twenty-four years. After twenty-four years, all they had was Ishmael, a son of conflict. Now God had blessed Abraham and Sarah with Isaac, a promised son.

Galatians 4:22-23 identifies Ishmael as the son born after the flesh and Isaac as the son born after the promise. Ishmael was a human attempt to bring the fulfillment of God's promise. Isaac was God's fulfillment of his promise. How often do we settle for an immediate solution? Abraham did that when he chose to father his son Ishmael with his wife's handmaid. It's the same in our lives when we make hasty choices because of our impatience instead of waiting on God's timing. But there is a better way. When we align our desires with God, He will be faithful to His promise, just like when Sarah gave birth to their son Isaac.

MOSES' FAITH WAS SHAKEN BECAUSE OF HIS ANGER

Moses appears eight hundred fifty-one times in the Bible, and in the New Testament, his name is mentioned nearly as often as King David. Acts 7:20-22 gives us the following profile of Moses:

- He was strikingly handsome
- He was raised in royalty as a prince in Egypt
- He grew up surrounded by the plentiful resources of Egypt
- He was educated in all the wisdom of the Egyptians

Even though Moses had everything he needed to be successful, he had an anger issue that cost him dearly. On three occasions, Moses' outburst of anger has direct negative consequences for him.

Moses' first outburst derailed him. In Exodus 2:11-15, Moses witnessed an Egyptian beating an enslaved Israelite. He came to the man's defense and ended up killing the Egyptian. The next day Moses saw two Israelite men fighting and tried to break it up. One of the men asked him, "Who are you to be a ruler over us? Are you going kill me as you killed that Egyptian yesterday?" Word got out concerning Moses' action, and when Pharaoh heard about the murder, he ordered Moses to be arrested and killed. In fear for his life, Moses fled Egypt and lived as a foreigner in a region known as Midian. There, he married a woman named Zipporah, whose father hired him as a shepherd. Moses, the one-time Prince of Egypt, took a job that had no prestige or privilege. There, in place, the Bible describes as the "backside of the desert" near Mount Sinai, he hid from the bustling crowds of Egypt for the next forty years.

The following display of Moses' anger is mentioned in Exodus 32. Moses descended Mount Sinai, where he spent many days alone with God. During this time, God had given him the Ten Commandments. While Moses was on the mountain, the

Israelites made a golden calf to worship. When Moses saw the Israelites worshipping and dancing before the golden calf, he angrily threw down and shattered the two tablets inscribed with God's commands. What Moses had received privately with God was broken publicly because of his anger. Even in our lives, how often is a word from The Lord lost because of anger?

The third instance I want to point out is in Numbers 20, where we read that Israel was wandering in the wilderness and needed water. Tensions were high, and Moses was frustrated because of the people's constant murmuring and complaining. It probably seemed to him that nothing could please them. God instructed Moses to speak to a rock and command water to come out of it. At Moses' word, enough water would come out of the rock to satisfy all the people and their livestock. By the time Moses and Aaron got everyone in place and the stage set for this great miracle, Moses was so angry with them that he struck the rock twice with his staff instead of speaking to it as the Lord had instructed him. Moses' anger caused him to disobey the Lord. God, in His great mercy, allowed water to flow from the rock and meet Israel's water needs anyway. However, God spoke to Moses again, saying, "Because you struck the rock when I said speak to the rock, you will not lead them to the Promise Land" (v. 20)

In all three examples, the people were wrong. The Egyptian was in the wrong for beating the enslaved Israelite servant. The Israelites were also in the wrong when they built a golden calf and worshiped it. Finally, the Israelites were wrong for the constant complaining and murmuring in the wilderness. But you can't let people make you upset and angry, even if their behavior is inappropriate. You will be the loser.

One of the first steps in controlling your temper is realizing that you are not responsible for people's actions but for your response to their actions. Anger is a human emotion everyone experiences. It is not a sin to be angry. It is a sin to let your anger get out of control. Ephesians 4:26-27, "Don't sin by letting anger gain control over you. Don't let the sun go down while you are still angry, for anger gives a mighty foothold to the devil." Uncontrolled anger does so much damage. Moses' anger isolated him in a desert, caused him to break the tablets containing the Ten Commandments, and disqualified him from being able to enter the Promise Land along with the rest of the Hebrew people. These instances may seem too harsh today, but we must remember that all this happened under the Old Covenant that the Bible describes as obsolete in Hebrews 8:13. In I Corinthians 10:11, Paul wrote, "Now all these things happened to them as examples...."

ELIJAH'S FAITH WAS SHAKEN BECAUSE OF INTIMIDATION

Elijah was a great prophet and a man of faith. It was with the spirit of Elijah that John the Baptist would later prepare the way for the coming earthly ministry of Jesus. God powerfully used Elijah. Still, he was just a man. In I Kings 17 & 18, The Bible describes several amazing things that God did for His prophet Elijah.

During a long drought, God told Elijah to go to a brook called Cherith. While he was there, God used ravens to bring the prophet breakfast every morning and food at dinner time. In another instance, God used Elijah to prophesy over a small portion of flour and oil that a widow in a town called Zarephath thought would be her last meal. Because she obeyed the prophet's word, The Lord replenished her bin of flour and her jar of oil until the drought ended. Later, when he learned that the same widow's son had become sick and died, Elijah prayed for the boy, laid down over him, and brought him to life. Elijah prayed down fire on Mount Carmel and killed all the prophets of the false god Baal. Then Elijah prayed for rain after a three-year drought and a tremendous rainstorm came.

In these two chapters, Elijah is the man! But in chapter 19, we find that wicked King Ahab told his wife, Queen Jezebel, what Elijah had done to the prophets of Baal. Jezebel became furious and sent a messenger to Elijah, saying, "I will find you and do what you did to my prophets in the next twenty-four hours," (v.2). Uncharacteristically, Elijah panicked and ran for an entire day into the desert because of fear. Eventually, he came to a Juniper tree and sat beneath it. At some point, Elijah started believing it was his responsibility to fix everything. In doing so, he became emotionally burned out. Finally, he told God he'd had enough. He wanted his life to end, so he asked God to take him.

Elijah was shaken off course because of the intimidating message from Queen Jezebel. Scripture tells us that she was an evil woman. She dominated her weak husband and manipulated people and events to fit her desires. She and King Ahab had a group of false prophets. Together, they worshiped the idol, Baal.

On the other hand, Elijah was a faithful prophet of God Almighty. He was God's man in a time of famine and national distress, and God was not about to allow His prophet to fade to black because he was burned out. The Lord gave Elijah instructions. He told Elijah to a brook called Cherith, and the ravens fed him there. Let's turn to the Bible narrative and read what happened next.

Eventually, the brook ran dry because there had been no rain. When Elijah regained his strength, the Lord directed him to a place called Zarephath. There, he met a widow who, even though she had little, prepared him some food. Because she obeyed and trusted the Lord, her meal bucket overflowed for many days. Once again, when Elijah went to Mount Carmel, he had a word from the Lord, and he prayed down fire upon the altar. In all three of these situations, Elijah had a direct word from the Lord, and he received a miracle at each place. Notice, however, that in chapter 19, Elijah never received a word from the Lord to go to the desert. He ran there because he was intimidated by the words of Jezebel. He allowed that intimidation to push him off course into a desert where the Lord had never directed him. The good news is that when Elijah was off course, God knew where he was; under a tree. He knew what he needed; to eat. He knew how to get it to him; God sent an angel.

Certain situations are intimidating to any of us. At times like this, it's easy to react out of fear and find ourselves out of the will of God. If intimidation has gotten you off course, remember that God knows where you are too. He also knows what you need and how to get it to you!

JOB'S FAITH WAS SHAKEN BECAUSE OF HIS PAIN

Job's life was painfully altered by losing his children, wealth, and health.

It was so painful that even his wife told him he should give up, curse God, and die. I'm not attacking Job's wife. You have to keep in mind that Mrs. Job buried ten children also. The painful realization of her loss and Job's horrendous suffering led her to believe the only way out was to end it.

Job's pain was so intense that he said in Job 6:2-3, If all his pain could be put on scales, it would be "heavier than all the sand of the sea." Job's pain led him to question the day he was born and ask, "Why wasn't I taken from my mother's womb to the grave? Why wasn't I born dead? I should have been a stillborn baby" (Job 3:11)!

Learning how to handle pain is one of life's greatest lessons. Our personal pain can be destructive if we don't understand this lesson. So many Christians focus on their present experience instead of the eternal perspective. 2 Corinthians 4:17-18 reads, "For our present troubles are quite small and won't last very long. Yet they produce for us an immeasurably great glory that will last forever! So we don't look at the troubles we can see right now: rather, we look forward to what we have not yet seen. For the troubles we see will soon be over, but the joys to come will last forever." In other words, God is using my temporary pain now to prepare me for the eternal. He doesn't waste a hurt, trial, or disappointment. He can take negatives and bring positives out of them. Romans 8:18 teaches us, "What we suffer now is nothing compared to the glory He will give us later."

DAVID'S FAITH WAS SHAKEN BECAUSE OF HIS LUST

In II Samuel 11, David sent the Israelite army to war with the Ammonites. David was known as a masterful warrior and successfully went to battle. It was his custom to go with his military to the battlefield. However, he decided to stay home this time instead of going into battle with his men. This wrong decision led him to make other bad decisions, which would have negative ramifications for the rest of his life. By staying home, he was not acting in his position as King of Israel. Unfortunately, this dilemma is not unique to King David. Many people have fallen to the temptation of lust because they were out of their appointed place.

One night from the roof of his palace, David noticed a beautiful woman bathing. As he watched, her lustful passions started to stir inside him. David sent one of his servants to inquire about her and learned her name was Bathsheba, the wife of Uriah the Hittite. The King knew that her husband was on the battlefield. So David sent for her to be brought to his palace, where they had sex. The bad choice to stay home led to the sinful decision to commit adultery. Lust can cause good people to do evil things!

Later, Bathsheba contacted David and informed him that she was pregnant. Upon learning this, David began to scheme ways to get rid of Bathsheba's husband, Uriah. David sent word to Joab, the captain of his army. He asked him to send Uriah home to David. When Uriah was ushered into the King's chamber, David asked Uriah about Joab and the battle in general. Afterward, David instructed Uriah to go home, thinking he would have sex with Bathsheba and Uriah would think the baby was his. David even sent a gift along and urged Uriah to relax and have his feet washed. But Uriah was a man of principle and decided to sleep outside on a mat near his front door. When David inquired of Uriah, Uriah said something like this, "How can I sleep with my wife when the Ark of God is held by the enemy, and my captain and brothers are on the battlefield? I can't do that" (v.11). David's scheme wasn't working, so he invited Uriah to have dinner and plied him with wine until he was drunk, thinking that would do the trick. But Uriah slept outside with his servants again.

Finally, David wrote a letter, sealed it, and gave it to Uriah to take to Captain Joab. The letter commanded Joab to put Uriah on the front line of battle. The faithful soldier Uriah carried the instructions of his demise from the unfaithful King. Shortly after, David received word from the field that the fighting was severe, and Uriah was killed. David, now cold-hearted, told the servant to tell Joab that "these things happen. It could have been anyone. Don't let this upset you" (v.25).

Another horrible decision! Adultery, and now murder. Once David started making bad decisions, they just kept getting worse and worse. With Uriah gone, David married Bathsheba, and she gave birth to their son. II Samuel 11:27 describes how God felt about David's decisions: "But the Lord was very displeased with what David had done."

"So the LORD sent Nathan the prophet to tell David this story: "There were two men in a certain town. One was rich, and one was poor. The rich man owned a great many sheep and cattle. The poor man owned nothing but one little lamb he had bought. He raised that little lamb and it grew up with his children. It ate from the man's plate and drank from his cup. He cuddled it in his arms like a baby daughter. One day a guest arrived at the home of the wealthy man. But instead of killing an animal from his flock or herd, he took the poor man's lamb and killed it and prepared it for his guest" (II Samuel 12:1-4).

David was furious! He was so angry that he commanded that the rich farmer should die, but only after he had repaid the poor farmer with four lambs in place of the one he had taken because he did this thing with no pity.

That's when Nathan responded, "You are the man!" The simple illustration spoke directly to David and opened his eyes to his guilt. The purpose of confrontation is to open our eyes to the truth. David had been blinded by his lust, and now the truth revealed his sin. God often confronts us with His Word and Holy Spirit to open our eyes to our sins and failures. Listen to the full force of God's disappointment with David because of this situation in verses 7-9: "You are that man! The LORD, the God of Israel, says: I anointed you king of Israel and saved you from the power of Saul. I gave you your master's house and his wives and the kingdoms of Israel and Judah. And if that had not been enough, I would have given you much, much more. Why, then, have you despised the word of the LORD and done this horrible deed? For you have murdered Uriah the Hittite with the sword of the Ammonites and stolen his wife."

No doubt shocked by the frontal assault of truth, the prophet then announced to David that there would be consequences for his sin. First, verses 9-10, "Why have you despised the commandment of the Lord, to do evil in His sight? You have killed Uriah the Hittite with the sword; you have taken his wife to be your wife, and have killed him with the sword of the people of Ammon. Now therefore, the sword shall never depart from your house, because you have despised Me, and have taken the wife of Uriah the Hittite to be your wife."

Even though it is an inevitable part of life, most of us dislike conflict. Some people will go to great lengths to avoid it. Others will attempt to make accommodations so everyone can just get along. Even those who use conflict as a means of manipulating others wouldn't want continual conflict among their own family. It's hard to imagine to utter shame that David must have felt when he heard this edict. For the rest of King David's life, there would be a family war. David's family became known for their turmoil, hatred, violence, and dysfunction.

Then in verses 11-12, "Thus says the Lord: 'Behold, I will raise adversity against you from your own house; and I will take your wives before your eyes and give them to your neighbor, and he shall lie with your wives in the sight of this sun. For you did it secretly, but I will do this thing before all Israel, before the sun."

The idea that all of Israel would see the consequence of David's flagrant disobedience is nearly overwhelming. It might seem to us that God would cover for David, shield him from the consequences and embarrassment, and discipline him in private. But no, God had great plans for David. He also had a special love for him as His anointed. God, however, had set a precedent with King Saul, and as much as He loved David, He wouldn't change course. The Kingship was too special to be abused. Too much was at stake, but God was not yet finished.

A third painful consequence is found in verses 14-17, "'However because by this deed you have given great occasion to the enemies of the Lord to blaspheme, the child also who is born to you shall surely die.' Then Nathan departed to his house. And the Lord struck the child that Uriah's wife bore to David, and it became ill. David, therefore, pleaded with God for the child, and David fasted and went in and lay all night on the ground. So the elders of his house arose and went to him, to raise him from the ground. But he would not, nor did he eat food with them. Then on the seventh day, it came to pass that the child died...."

David began with such promise but was brought to his

knees by his reckless desires. The consequences of David's sin were not intended to disqualify him but to lead him back to the right path. David was not just some random shepherd. He was God's chosen shepherd for His chosen people. God wanted David to return, or he potentially risked leading the entire nation astray. God corrects every child He receives, Hebrews 12:6 says. God's correction is proof of His love. His aim is restoration. Amid Nathan's message of correction from God, David seeks forgiveness. He admits his sorrow. No doubt, he wanted to know that God was still there and that He still loved him. In verse 13, we read, "So David said to Nathan, 'I have sinned against the Lord.'" Confession is an acknowledgment of error and a plea to be pardoned for sin. In the New Testament, Paul wrote, "For godly sorrow produces repentance leading to salvation" (II Corinthians 7:10). Only after David's confession does Nathan pronounce, "The Lord has forgiven you" (verse 13). What awesome news for David! Especially when he hears Nathan say in the last part of that verse, "You shall not die."

God's forgiveness is the greatest experience in life. David wrote about experiencing God's forgiveness in Psalm 32:1, "Oh, what joy for those whose rebellion is forgiven." David was a guilty man but experienced the joy of being pardoned or released from his crimes. God didn't forgive David because David deserved it. God forgave David because God is faithful. "If we confess our sins, He is faithful and just to forgive us our sins, and to cleanse us from all unrighteousness" (1 John 1:9).

SIMON PETER'S FAITH WAS SHAKEN BECAUSE OF HIS FAILURE

The night before his crucifixion, Jesus knew Simon Peter was about to be severely tested and warned him, "And the Lord said, "Simon, Simon! Indeed, Satan has asked for you, that he may sift you as wheat. But I have prayed for you, that your faith should not fail; and when you have returned to Me, strengthen your brethren" (Luke 22:31,32). Peter's response was somewhat prideful, "But he said to Him, 'Lord, I am ready to go with You, both to prison and to death'" (v.33). But that very night, under the pressure of Jesus' arrest, surrounded by a hostile crowd, Peter's faith was shaken with three denials. Peter's arrogance set him up for a fall. "Then He said, 'I tell you, Peter, the rooster shall not crow this day before you will deny three times that you know Me'" (v34).

Peter came face to face with failure. Sooner or later, we all do. "For we all have sinned; all fall short of God's glorious standard" (Romans 3:23 NLT). Failure is something we all have in common. We have all come up short, missed the mark, and fallen flat on our faces. In some way, at some time, we have all experienced failure. In John 21, Jesus restored Peter. Jesus took a man who had a major defeat and put him through the process of restoration. In Acts 2, Peter was in the Upper Room and received the Holy Spirit. When there was confusion in Jerusalem as to what was happening, Peter quoted the prophet Joel concerning the Holy Spirit and preached about Jesus' death, burial, and resurrection. Three thousand souls believed his word and were baptized (Acts 2:41). Now that is faith restored after being shaken by failure!

JOHN THE BAPTIST'S FAITH WAS SHAKEN BECAUSE OF AN OFFENSE

John the Baptist was the forerunner of Jesus, (Matthew 3:1-3). Jesus approached a baptism service in the Jordan River that John the Baptist was conducting. John stopped the service and shouted, "Behold the Lamb of God who takes away the sins of the world" (John 1:29). Jesus requested for John the Baptist to baptize him, but John was reluctant and stated he was not even worthy to untie the straps of Jesus' sandals (John 1:27). When John baptized Jesus he witnessed the heavens opening, the Holy Spirit descending like a dove landing on Jesus, and the Father declaring, "This is My beloved Son, in whom I am well pleased" (Matthew 3:16-17). What an incredible experience that had to be for John the Baptist, the cousin of Jesus!

Luke 7:18-20 tells the story of John the Baptist in prison. Even though John had baptized Jesus and witnessed the signs from heaven, he was still uncertain if Jesus was the promised Messiah. After all, his life was on the line. It's one thing to be certain when you are preaching before a crowd watching the heavens as you baptize the lamb of God. It's an entirely different matter when a ruler has called for your head.

It is in this precarious circumstance that John sent two of his disciples to Jesus with a single question, "Are you the messiah we've been expecting, or should we keep looking for someone else" (v.20)? John the Baptist goes from declaring Jesus to be the Lamb of God, to asking if He was the Messiah. How did that happen? The answer is in verse 23 when Jesus responded to John the Baptist's disciples saying, "Tell John God blesses those who are not offended by me." The forerunner of Jesus was dealing with an offense. He had been arrested and put in prison. He no longer had the freedom to publicly conduct his ministry. His voice had been silenced, and he was offended. It is out of offense he questioned who Jesus is.

Historians have indicated that King Herod Antipas had an affair with his brother's wife, Herodias, while his brother, Phillip, was visiting Rome. Herodias divorced Phillip and married King Herod. John the Baptist denounced their marriage, (Matthew 14:4). Herodias was furious, and wanted John the Baptist executed (Mark 6:19). King Herod believed John the Baptist was a righteous man, and liked to listen to him speak (Mark 6:20). To appease Herodias, King Herod locked John the Baptist up in prison, but would not execute him because he was afraid of the people who believed John the Baptist was a prophet, (Matthew 14:5).

John the Baptist's ministry started gloriously and powerfully. He was a powerful voice and a popular prophet. Now he is locked up in a filthy prison cell all because of a manipulative woman, and eventually lost his life because of her. While in prison he was overtaken by his offense, and doubts began to prevail in his mind and caused him to ask the question, "Is Jesus the Messiah, or should we look for another?" His faith was shaken!

We've examined seven men whose faith was shaken because of impatience, anger, intimidation, pain, lust, failure, and offense. Doesn't that sound familiar? Isn't it amazing how many people are dealing with these seven issues today? Here is what we learn from these men who dealt with some tough issues, and were shaken in their faith:

SHAKEN DOES NOT MEAN YOU ARE DESTROYED

What shook you doesn't have to destroy you. There is a big difference between being defeated and being destroyed. Paul wrote these reassuring words in 2 Corinthians 4:8-9, "We are pressed on every side by troubles, but we are not crushed and broken. We are perplexed, but we don't give up and quit. We are hunted down, but God never abandons us. We get knocked down, but we get up again and keep going."

Defeat is being knocked down. Destroyed is staying down. Proverbs 24:16 teaches us, "For though the righteous fall seven times, they rise again." We may have our defeats, but we are not destroyed. We can rise again because the one who rose again from the dead on the third day lives within us.

SHAKEN DOES NOT MEAN GOD GIVES UP ON YOU

He continues to work in us even when our faith is shaken, "Being confident of this, that he who began a good work in you will carry it on to completion until the day of Christ Jesus" (Philippians 1:6). God never stops working in your life! Psalm

103:14 tells us that, "He knows our frame: He remembers that we are but dust." The phrase, "He knows our frame," means He knows we're human. The God who created us knows we are nowhere near perfect, and He patiently works with us. He knows our weaknesses, our struggles, our insecurities, our failures, and our limitations, and still never gives up on us! We use to sing a song in Children's Church entitled, "He's Still Working On Me." The chorus went like this:

"He's still working on me
To make me what I need to be
It took him just a week
to make the moon and the stars.
The Sun and the Earth, Jupiter, and Mars.
How loving and patient He must be
'Cause He still workin' on me" (Joel Hemphill)

SHAKEN DOES NOT MEAN YOU CANNOT TRY AGAIN

Many victories in life have come after trying again. You are stronger and wiser now. You've learned some hard lessons and you still have the possibility of overcoming defeat if you try again. You're more qualified than ever. "Don't be afraid to start over again. This time you're not starting from scratch, you're starting from experience." (Author Unknown)

Listen to Michael Jordan, the greatest basketball player in the history of the game: "I've missed more than 9,000 shots in my career. I've lost almost 300 games. 26 times, I've been trusted to take the game-winning shot and missed. I've failed over and over and over again in my life. And that is why I succeed." (https://www.forbes.com/quotes/11194/).

It is amazing how God blessed each of these men whose faith had been shaken:

After Abraham became impatient and fathered Ishmael, God still blessed him with his promised son, Issac (Genesis 21:1-3). Moses certainly had his anger issues, yet we read, There was never another prophet like Moses whom God used to perform mighty miracles for all of Israel to see, (Deuteronomy 34:10-12).

Elijah is known for his depression, intimidation, and isolation from dealing with Jezebel (I Kings 19). Yet, later on, Elisha saw how greatly the Spirit of God worked through Elijah and wanted the same for himself so that he could fulfill God's purpose for his life. Before Elijah was taken to heaven, he asked Elisha what he could do for him. Elisha requested for a double portion of Elijah's mighty spirit to be upon him. (2 Kings 2:9)

God blessed Job with twice as much of everything he had at the beginning of his story at the end of his story (Job 42:10). God gave Job double for his trouble!

David, the man after God's own heart (1 Samuel 13:14) made a bad decision, which led to a sinful decision and a dreadful one. All these decisions were the result of lust. When David gave himself over to lust, his world fell apart. When the Prophet Nathan confronted David, he confessed his sin and received God's great forgiveness.

Jesus restored Peter, filled him with the Spirit, and anointed him to be the spokesperson on the Day of Pentecost with three thousand believing in Christ (Acts 2:41).

After John the Baptist questioned if Christ was the Messiah, Jesus publicly affirmed him, stating there had never been one greater than John (Luke 7:28).

Each of these men had their issues and struggles. They experienced a time in their lives when their faith was shaken. Yet, the good news is that God never gave up on them. The Lord continued to work patiently with them and bless them. God will do the same for you even if your faith has been shaken!

CHAPTER 3

LIFE IS NOT ALWAYS FAIR

Life can hit hard and doesn't always play by the rules. Sports fans know that every sport has guidelines, regulations, and boundaries so that the game can be played at its very best. Then there are referees, umpires, and judges to oversee the game, and enforce the sport's rules and regulations. The out-of-bounds call, the offsides call, and the personal foul call, were all made to ensure that the game is fair, and is as competitive as possible. While this is true in the sports world, in the real world the rules of life are not always followed, and often there is no one there to enforce the regulations.

At some time in life, everyone deals with something that wasn't fair. As a pastor, one of the statements I've heard the most in counseling people was, "It's just not fair!" The hard truth is that nowhere in the Bible does it say life is always going to be fair. Jesus never taught life would be fair. Here are a few of Jesus' statements that let you know life is not always going to be fair.

"If anyone slaps you on the right cheek, turn to them the other cheek also." Matthew 5:39

"Love your enemies! Pray for those who persecute you!" Matthew 5:44

"The Father causes his sun to rise on the evil and the good and sends rain on the righteous and unrighteous." Matthew 5:45

"The poor you will always have with you." Matthew 26:11

"In this world, you will have trouble." John 16:33

What's fair about any of these statements? Do I have to turn the other cheek? I don't get to retaliate? That's not fair! I have to love and pray for my enemies. I don't have a problem loving and praying for people who are nice to me, but now I have to pray for people who have hurt me. That's not fair! Evil people enjoy the same sunshine as good people, and both get rained on? That's not fair! In the law of economics, not everyone is going to be wealthy. There's always going to be poverty in this world. That's not fair! Jesus promised me trouble. Well, that's one promise He has kept. That's not fair!

In Luke 10:25-37 Jesus tells the story of how a man was treated very unfairly while traveling from Jerusalem to Jericho. Thugs attacked him, robbed him, beat him up, and left him half dead on the side of the road. To get the full impact of this crime we need to examine the crime scene. Crime scenes are places of loss where someone was robbed, injured, or murdered. Such scenes can be horrendous to look upon, yet trained investigators will comb every inch of a crime scene searching for evidence or clues that might bring answers to what happened. This is critically important to solving the crime, and finding those responsible for the crime to hold them accountable. As we analyze the crime scene in Luke 10 we can learn much about life. Here's what we find out about the man who was attacked on his journey to Jericho:

HE LOST FINANCIALLY

The thieves robbed him of his money. When thieves come they are always looking for valuables. They don't waste their time on petty, and inexpensive things. Thieves rob banks, hack accounts, embezzle funds, steal credit cards, shoplift jewelry, take diamonds, and pickpocket wallets because of their monetary value. When the thieves took the man's money they stole from him that which was very valuable to him. His money was his livelihood. The loss could have a huge impact on his present and future. Financial loss is painful because of the negative effects it has on our lives. Such losses set us back, and restrict us from often achieving set financial goals.

HE LOST HIS DIGNITY

The thieves stripped him of his clothing. The word strip refers to the removal of a covering. He is now laying completely naked on the ground. With no covering over him, his body is exposed in total humiliation. The thieves didn't stop robbing him. They were intent on taking his self-esteem, and leaving him as disgraced as possible. Humiliation has to do with public shame, embarrassment, and the loss of self-respect. The man was laying on the side of the road with his clothing stripped off of him completely humiliated.

HE LOST PHYSICALLY

The thugs beat him, cut him, and kicked him until he was a bloody mess. He is beaten and left on the side of the road to die. He lost his self-sufficiency. He is laying in a powerless state. The thieves took his money, dignity, and now his health. For a man's sense of worth, these three components of life are very important. Every man desires to be in control of his world which includes finances, a healthy self-image, and physical health. To be able to stand on his own two feet, make his living, and provide for his family is a God-given desire men possess. The thieves were cruel in taking his self-sufficiency from him. Robbed, naked, and beaten on the side of the road means he isn't going to make it to his desired destination of Jericho.

HE SUFFERED EMOTIONALLY

As the man was laying on the side of the road a priest approached him. With the entrance of a priest into the crime scene there was hope for the man. However, when the priest saw the man's condition he passed by him and continued on his journey. Later, a Levite came by, saw the man, and went on his way. What makes this so troubling is who these two men were. The first was a priest. A priest is called by God and serves as a mediator between God and men. His chief duty is to bring people to God in prayer and worship. The Levite was a Temple assistant who was subordinate to the priest. He served in the daily operations of the Temple. Both of these men served important roles in the ministry of bringing people to God. Yet, when they come upon a wounded man on the side of the road they walked away saying nothing. No words of encouragement. No expressions of concern. No prayers. They just walked away. While they offered no verbal support, their silence spoke volumes. There is an old saying that goes like this, "When you say nothing, you're saying something." The priest and Levite passed by a wounded man as though he didn't even exist when it was their ministry to bring people to God. Their silence is deafening. Bishop T. D. Jakes said, "If you ever want to know who people are, watch and see how they treat people they think they don't need."

The priest and Levite made a bad situation even worse with their responses. These men represented spiritual authority, and for them to just walk away was cold and cruel. Walking past the hurting man and ignoring him was so insensitive. Now the man suffered emotionally from the rejection of the priest and Levite. Rejection is one of the most difficult emotions to deal with because it cuts to your core person. When people in spiritual authority reject you it just compounds the pain. Emotional pain can be far greater than financial loss, humiliation, or physical injury.

After the disappointing responses of the priest and Levite a Samaritan came by. His response was different from the priest's and Levite's. The Samaritan had compassion for the wounded man, gave him medical assistance, and took him to a safe place for his recovery. Also, he paid the bill for the wounded man's place to stay and returned later to follow up on his progress. Why was the Samaritan's response so different from the priest's and Levite's responses? The Samaritan saw the wounded man's value. He saw beyond the man's brokenness and nakedness. Sometimes you have to see beyond the now to recognize a person's value. If you've had brokenness and rejection in your life you still have value. The thieves who robbed the man took so much from him, but they couldn't take his value. You have value even if people don't see it. Your value does not decrease because of someone's inability to see your worth. Your value is not determined by how someone treated you. You may have been abandoned, betrayed, violated, offended, hurt, or used, but you still have value. I have used the illustration of taking a twenty-dollar bill in a sermon and talking about its value. Then I would wrinkle it up in my hand, put it on the floor, and stomp on it. Pick it up and show everyone how bad it looked. While it no longer looked like a new crisp twenty-dollar bill it still held its value! You can still purchase an item up to twenty dollars or less with it. That's how it is with us in God's eyes. No matter what you've been through you still have value!

The man who reached out to the wounded man laying on the side of the road was a Samaritan. The Samaritans were mixed nationalities of Jews and Gentiles who had settled in the city of Samaria. The Jews despised them and would have no dealings with them at all. The man who was attacked was a Jew. The priests and the Levites were Jews. In Jesus' story, you have a Samaritan reaching out to a Jew. Sometimes God goes outside your circle to bring restoration to you and work His plan for your life. Life is all about circles. Family circles. Church circles. Ministry Circles. Business circles. Circles of influence. Your circle of friends. When a Jewish Priest and Levite passed by a wounded Jewish man a Samaritan man from another circle took the time to minister to him.

As bad as it was for this wounded man he was only half dead. If you are half dead that means you are half alive! Half alive means your story is not over, and you still have hope, and a future. God can do amazing things with people who are half alive!

What this man experienced on his journey from Jerusalem to Jericho was certainly not fair. Being robbed was not fair.

Being stripped was not fair. Being beat up was not fair. Being passed by was not fair. Being left on the side of the road was not fair.

But that was not the end of his story! Don't get stuck on what wasn't fair. Don't let your world revolve around the unfairness that happened to you. Being controlled by who did you wrong or what didn't go your way is a terrible way to live. It will keep you half-dead. You don't want to live half-dead the rest of your life!

Keep in mind the wounded man recovered. You can't just focus on his loss, injuries, or rejection. His story has to include his recovery, and the fact that he overcame all the unfairness that happened to him. If all you focus on is what wasn't fair you will stay disappointed and frustrated. There are time-tested ways to help you cope if you feel you've been treated unfairly.

TRUST GOD WITH YOUR FUTURE

After Israel had been in slavery to the Babylonians for seventy years God spoke through the Prophet Jeremiah concerning their future, "For I know the plans I have for you. They are plans for good and not for disaster, to give you a future and a hope" (Jeremiah 29:11). The Lord spoke to a nation of people who had suffered through seventy years of slavery and said I have plans for you. God's plans gave Israel hope for a good future. The Babylonians had attacked and destroyed Jerusalem in 586 BC, and taken the surviving Israelites captive to Babylon. The Israelites had lost everything and became the possessions of the Babylonians. There is nothing fair about slavery. After seventy years of suffering God had great plans for people who had been treated unfairly! When dealing with unfairness, remember these words, "Trust in the Lord with all your heart, and lean not on your own understanding. In all your ways acknowledge him, and he shall direct your paths" (Proverbs 3:5-6).

KEEP YOUR ATTITUDE IN CHECK

Don't fall into the trap of thinking you are the only one who has ever been treated unfairly or gone through hard times. Everyone encounters them. James 1:2 says, "My brethren, count it all joy when you fall into various trials." The words "count" or "consider it all joy" have to do with attitude. James is telling us to keep the right attitude regardless of what type of difficulty we encounter. A negative or critical attitude keeps you defeated. A healthy attitude will help you rise above hard times or being done wrong.

The Apostle Paul had more than his fair share of hardships, sufferings, beatings, poverty, and sickness. Yes, the great Apostle Paul knew all about unfairness. While in a Roman prison, he wrote a brief letter to believers in Philippi. The dominant theme of Philippians is not sorrow, but joy. Paul uses the word joy or rejoices sixteen times. Joy is not just feeling happy all the time. It is much deeper than excitement or enthusiasm. It is much more than perfect circumstances. Joy is the pleasure that comes from the Lord's presence, or the fulfillment of accomplishing his purpose for your life. That's why Paul was on the inside of prison, writing to people on the outside of prison, telling them, "Rejoice in the Lord always, I will say it again: Rejoice" (Philippians 4:4)! This verse is all about attitude!

STRIVE TO BE AN EXAMPLE

What an amazing example Joseph is for us in Genesis chapters 37-50. He experienced some unfair things such as jealousy, deception, and betrayal. Joseph's journey included a pit which represents rejection, Potiphar's house which represents temptation, and prison which represents isolation on his way to Pharaoh's palace which represents promotion. With all Joseph encountered as a young man, he learned life is not always fair, but he also learned that God is always faithful. As it turned out, Joseph's story was more about what God did for him than what people did to him. What God did for Joseph was far greater than anything done to him. Genesis 39:2 tells us, "The Lord was with Joseph so that he prospered."

God blessed Joseph while he was going through rejection, betrayal, temptation, and isolation. As a result, he was promoted to serve as Governor of Egypt under Pharaoh. Yes, the blessing of the Lord brought him honor, but in addition, Joseph demonstrated remarkable strength of character. Despite facing animosity, rejection, and temptation, he chose to respond with love, blessings, and a firm "no". Even when he found himself alone or in a position of authority, he remained steadfast in his faith and commitment to serving others. Like Joseph, you can be an example of favor and wisdom for others to follow. "In everything set them an example by doing what is good" (Titus 2:7).

CHAPTER 4

REJECTION HURTS

In Hebrews 4:15, the author identifies Jesus as our High Priest "who understands our weaknesses, for He faced all of the same temptations we do, yet He did not sin." On earth, Jesus experienced hatred, betrayal, and rejection. If Jesus had not left Heaven and come to Earth He would have never experienced any of this negativity brought on to Him by people. But because He experienced it He understands it. Jesus can relate to rejection because He experienced people not liking Him, not believing Him, and not accepting Him. Isaiah prophesied this would happen in Isaiah 53:3, "He was despised and rejected." Peter also wrote about it in 1 Peter 2:24, "He was rejected by the people." Let's look more closely at these instances when Jesus was rejected.

KING HEROD THE GREAT

That King Herod might reject Jesus should surprise no one. Still, his outright refusal of acknowledgment bore great significance. Christianity.com describes King Herod as, "a shrewd and clever tyrant and a great builder. Today, roughly two thousand years later, the remains of his incredible structures, including his fortress of Masada, are still visible in Israel. He built Masada because he was afraid that someone would try to take his kingdom. He even had his sons executed because he perceived them as a threat to his kingdom. It was said in Herod's day, 'Better to be one of Herod's pigs than his sons.'" "Who Was King Herod the Great." Christianity.Com, 30 Sept. 2021, www.christianity.com/Jesus/birth-of-Jesus/roman-world/king-herod-then-and-now.html.

When Jesus was born in Bethlehem, a small village outside of Jerusalem, King Herod ruled over Israel. Word spread quickly of a newborn King for the Jewish people. When the news reached King Herod he became very upset. After being outsmarted by the Wise Men Herod immediately began plotting a plan to do away with the Christ child. Herod sent soldiers to kill every male child two years and under in and around Bethlehem. In a dream, an Angel appeared to Joseph instructing him to take Mary and baby Jesus and flee to Egypt. Joseph followed the angel's instructions and made the four-hundred-mile journey to Egypt which probably took them about a month to travel by donkey. They lived in Egypt for three years. When Herod died the Angel told Joseph they could return to Israel. Joseph and Mary returned to Nazareth where Jesus grew up. The massacre of innocent children shows how wicked King Herod was. It also reveals the extent Herod would go because he was threatened by the birth of Jesus.

HIS COUNTRYMEN

We might expect rejection from King Herod, but Jesus also faced rejection from His countrymen. John 1:11 reads, "Even in His own land, and among His own people, he was not accepted." Jesus did not fit the image of a King the Jews were looking for. He was born in a stable wrapped in rags to a young, poor couple who weren't even married! No royalty. No fame. No title. No palace. No throne. No crown. No prestige. No wealth. Jesus was rejected by His own people because He was not what they were looking for in a leader.

Not only was Jesus rejected by the Jewish leaders, but even His own community turned against Him. After Jesus began His public ministry He returned to His hometown of Nazareth to teach in the synagogue. The townspeople recognized Him as Joseph's son who worked in His father's carpenter shop. They saw Him grow up and were very familiar with His childhood. When the people heard Him teach they became so offended and outraged at his teachings that they attacked Him, and took Him to the edge of a cliff to throw Him off to kill Him. Amid the chaos and out-of-control mob, Jesus was able to escape, (Luke 4:14-30). The people of his hometown, Nazareth, rejected Jesus!

His brothers even turned on him. It was time for the Feast of Tabernacles in Judea, but Jesus was laying low in Galilee because the Jewish leaders were plotting His death. His brothers came to Him urging Him to go to the festival reasoning that He couldn't become a public figure hiding out like He was. They scoffed at Him to go perform miracles there because they didn't believe in Him. Jesus wouldn't go, and said to them, "My time has not yet come" (John 7:1-9). The brothers Jesus grew up with doubted Him, questioned Him, and rejected Him.

RELIGIOUS LEADERS

After Jesus drove the merchants from the Temple, He declared in Matthew 21:13, "My house shall be called the house of prayer, but you have turned it into a den of thieves." Then the religious leaders of that day came to Him questioning His authority to do such a thing. Jesus never backed down from them and He confronted their hypocrisy. They were angry and ready to arrest Jesus, but would not because Jesus had become so popular that they feared the huge crowds who believed He was a prophet, (Matthew 21:12-46). The religious leaders rejected his authority to put His house in order!

Jesus' followers consisted of observers, believers, as well as His disciples. At the beginning of John 6, Jesus performed the awesome miracle of multiplication by taking a little boy's lunch of five loaves of bread and two fish and feeding a multitude of people with it. According to John, the huge crowd consisted of five thousand men, plus women and children. The miracle was so great that the little boy's lunch not only provided a meal for the massive crowd but there were twelve baskets of bread left over. After the meal, everyone was full, and the people began to declare Jesus a prophet.

The next day, Jesus came back and the crowds were waiting to see Him. Then Jesus intensified His teaching by declaring that He was the "bread of life from heaven" (vv 32-35). Many in the crowd that day began to complain and disagree with His teaching. Even Jesus' disciples said this is hard to understand. It resulted in many of Jesus' followers deserting Him. Jesus asked His twelve disciples, "Are you leaving too" (John 6:67)? Isn't it amazing that when Jesus fed the multitude bread the people said He was a prophet? Yet, when He tried to teach them that He was the bread of life they left Him. So when Jesus ministered to the physical need of the people they received Him, but when he tried to minister to their spiritual needs they rejected Him.

JUDAS

Jesus chose Judas to be one of the twelve disciples. Judas traveled with Jesus, ate with Jesus, spent time with Jesus, heard Jesus teach, watched Jesus perform miracles, saw Jesus cast out devils, and witnessed Jesus heal the sick and even raise the dead. And after all of that, he still betrayed and rejected Jesus. How could he do it? Judas' rejection of Jesus began a long time before his kiss of betrayal in the Garden of Gethsemane. Jesus knew it, (John 6:64, 13:11), saw it in his heart, (13:21-27), and spoke of it before it ever happened, (Matthew 26:2, 20-25; Luke 22:3-4; John 6:70-71, 13:21-30). Judas's betrayal of Jesus is recorded in Matthew 26:14-16, 47-50. His rejection included a payment of thirty pieces of silver which he soon regretted. Judas rejected Jesus, and it turned out to be a horrific decision that led to his suicide.

PUBLIC OPINION

After Jesus was arrested in the Garden of Gethsemane, He stood trial the next morning before the Roman Governor Pilate. It was the governor's custom to release one prisoner each year during the Passover celebration. That year, there was a notorious criminal in prison named, Barabbas. As the crowds gathered before Pilate's house that morning he asked, "Which of the two (Jesus or Barabas) do you want me to release to you? The crowd shouted "Barabbas!" Pilate asked the crowd, "'What then shall I do with Jesus who was called Christ?' But they cried out all the more, 'Let Him be crucified!' Then the governor said, 'Why, what evil has He done?' But they cried out all the more, saying, 'Let Him be crucified!'" The public rejected an innocent man and accepted a guilty man that day (Matthew 27:11-26).

HIS HEAVENLY FATHER

Jesus' crucifixion began on that Friday at 9:00 a.m. with His body being nailed to a cross for six hours. After hanging for the first three hours in the morning sun, something unusual happened. Normally, noontime is when the sun shines at its brightest. But on this Friday, everything went dark, and Jesus hung in darkness for the next three hours. What caused the darkness? Could it have been that the Father could no longer bare to watch His only begotten Son suffer the cruelty and brutality of the cross, and turned His back? Crucifixion was the worst of deaths. Isaiah Chapter 53 compared crucifixion to the slaughtering of sheep. The darkness took Jesus' suffering to a whole new level. Darkness was a form of rejection Jesus had never known. Jesus was acquainted with rejection. He knew what it was like to have people reject Him. Yet, the pain of the Father's rejection was far greater than any rejection Jesus had ever experienced. It was in the darkness that Jesus screamed out with a loud voice, "My God, My God, why have you forsaken me" (Matthew 27:46)? In the darkness, Jesus felt completely isolated from His Heavenly Father. It wasn't long after this that Jesus gave up His spirit and died. Why did Jesus do it? Jesus experienced the rejection of the Father so that you and I could experience the acceptance of the Father.

Nobody likes rejection, yet it is unavoidable. The boyfriend who breaks up with his girlfriend. The young lady who didn't get into the sorority she so desperately wanted to be part of. The athlete who didn't make the team. The applicant who didn't get the job. The employee who was let go from the company. The candidate who lost the election. The betrayed spouse. The child who is abandoned by a parent. The parent who is rejected by a child.

Learning how to deal with rejection is one of the major keys to winning in life. If not, the lingering effects of it can last for years. I remember counseling a young man who was in his thirties whose father had abandoned him and his mother when he was three years old. He told me how after his father left he never had anything to do with him. His father never reached out to him at Christmas, his birthday, or school events. His father never gave financial assistance to help raise him, and his mother sometimes had to work two jobs to make it. As he told me his story he broke down and cried, and I could feel the pain of his rejection that he had lived with for over thirty years. I prayed with him, cried with him, and told him that his earthly father may have rejected him, but his Heavenly Father would never reject him.

Rejection destroys self-esteem leaving a person believing they're, "not good enough" or they, "don't fit in." Depression and withdrawal usually follow. Isolation becomes their norm as they convince themselves that is the best way to deal with the pain of their rejection. They become highly sensitive to criticism and have difficulties maintaining healthy relationships. Issues such as anger, guilt, shame, and drama can come from rejection if not properly dealt with. There is even a behavioral disorder called "Rejection-Sensitive Dysphoria." The word dysphoria comes from a Greek word that means "hard to bear." Rejection can certainly be hard to bear and it can cause us to be overly sensitive, preventing needed healthy relationships with other people. In overcoming rejection a person has to deal with themselves and not the person who rejected them. The person who rejected them made a choice. Now, the one who is rejected has to make a choice. We can't control another person's choices, but we can, and must, control our choices. When rejected, we must ask ourselves, will I let it destroy me or develop me? Will I let rejection be a dead-end or a new direction? The choice is ours!

Jesus experienced rejection from the time of His birth until His death, and He never let it keep Him from fulfilling His purpose. Don't allow rejection to keep you from fulfilling your purpose!

To overcome rejection you have to be a secure person. If not, rejection will produce many insecurities. As a Christian, your security is in Christ. Colossians 2:10 teaches us that we are complete in Christ. So all that I need I can find in Jesus. We have three basic needs to be secure believers so that we can put rejection behind us and move on in life to fulfill our destiny and purpose. Here are those three needs that we find in Christ:

BASIC NEED NUMBER ONE IS ACCEPTANCE

In Ephesians 1:6, Paul stated: "To the praise of the glory of His grace, by which He made us accepted in the Beloved. The word Beloved is referring to Jesus. God called Jesus His Beloved before he entered into ministry, preached a sermon, performed a miracle, or healed a person. In Mark 1:9-11, John the Baptist was baptizing Jesus in the Jordan River and God affirmed him saying, "This is my beloved Son, and I am fully pleased with you." God called Jesus his beloved again at the Mount of Transfiguration in Matthew 17:5.

There are four forms of love: Agape (God's love), Eros (romantic love), Storge (family love), and Philia (brotherly love). Agape is the highest form of love, and it is described in 1 Corinthians 13. This is the kind of love that makes us Beloved. Jesus has many titles in the scripture: savior, King, Lord, master, teacher, and healer, to name a few. Now though, Jesus has a new title that is an expression of the Father's love; Beloved.

When we come to Jesus He accepts us and calls us "Beloved," with the same love the Father gave Him. Everyone in Christ shares in this title. It means that we are now part of the family of God and citizens of the Kingdom of God. Ephesians

1:6 says, "We are accepted in the Beloved," which, in essence, means that we are blessed and highly favored.

Acceptance into the Beloved is not based on us, but on Jesus, and His love for us. It is the Agape Love which is the greatest of all the loves. John 15:13 says, "Greater love has no one than this: to lay down one's life for one's friends." You never have to worry about being good enough with this kind of love. That's why Jesus said in John 6:37, "The one who comes to me I will by no means cast out (reject)." Jesus didn't reject blind Bartimaeus, the sinful woman at Simon's house, Zacchaeus the Tax Collector, the woman at the well, or the thief on the cross, and He would never reject you from being in the Beloved.

BASIC NEED NUMBER TWO IS BELONGING

Adoption is a beautiful event. It is a great cause for celebration when children who are estranged from their birth parents are welcomed into a new home. Adoption provides children with new parents, a new family, a new name, a new beginning, and a new future. Full legal standing gives adopted children the same rights and responsibilities as birth children. Of all the benefits adopted children receive the greatest is the blessing of belonging. Foster children often go from home to home, but adoption means permanent residency. Everyone needs a place to belong, and a place to call home.

We see the beautiful scene of adoption in the scripture with God adopting us as His children at the time of our salvation. Ephesians 1:5 reads, "God decided in advance to adopt us into His own family by bringing us to himself through Jesus Christ." Likewise, Galatians 4:5 tells us, "God sent Him (Jesus) to buy freedom for us who were slaves to the law so that He could adopt us as His very own children." And again in Romans 8:15, "So you have not received a spirit that makes you fearful slaves. Instead, you received God's Spirit when He adopted you as His children."

One Sunday morning, I noticed a new family who were visiting our church for the first time. Little did I know, that meeting this family would be one of the greatest experiences of my pastoral ministry. They had just moved to our city from another state because of his job transfer. They were a wonderful Christian couple with two young daughters. They shared their story with me as I became better acquainted with them. It was as follows: They were married for ten years and were unable to conceive a child. They adopted a child after going to several doctors and receiving the same negative report. Their oldest daughter was adopted. A little over a year after the adoption, they learned they were pregnant and gave birth to their youngest daughter. To their amazement, the two girls even looked alike. As their pastor, I never saw them show partiality in any way to either daughter. They loved the adopted daughter and provided for her like the birth daughter! Adoption is beautiful!

When we ask God to forgive us, we experience what the Bible calls salvation. Salvation opens the door to God's family, who gives everyone a place to belong.

BASIC NEED NUMBER THREE IS KNOWING

As a Christian, you develop a lifestyle of living by what you know (faith) and not what you feel. Feelings change: they come and go. By feelings, I mean our emotions are not always trustworthy. Negative feelings can produce insecurity, while faith reveals confidence. Confidence begets strength, and strong believers stand firm amid adversity and difficulties because they are confident in the fundamentals of the Christian faith. They know God is alive; "I know that my redeemer lives" (Job 19:15). They know God is working for their good; "We know that in all things God works for the good of those who love Him, who have been called according to His purpose" (Romans 8:28). They also know that God completes what He starts; "Being confident of this, that He who began a good work in you will carry it on to completion until the day of Christ Jesus," (Philippians 1:6). They have a conviction that God is their provider, "My God will meet all your needs according to the riches of His glory in Christ Jesus" (Philippians 4:19). Because of these things, they know that their future is secure, "For I know the plans I have for you, says the Lord. They are plans for good and not for disaster, to give you a future and a hope" (Jeremiah 29:11).

By faith, they know that God answers prayer, "This is the confidence we have in approaching God: that if we ask anything according to his will, he hears us. And if we know He hears us, whatever we ask, we know that we have what we ask for" (1 John 5:14-15). Finally, they know Heaven is a real place; "Do not let your hearts be troubled. You believe in God, believe also in me. My Father's house has many rooms; if it were not so, would I have told you that I am going there to prepare a place for you? And if I go and prepare a place for you, I will come back and take you to be with me that you also may be where I am" (John 14:1-3).

The best way to overcome rejection is through Jesus Christ. In Jesus, we find acceptance (we are accepted into the Beloved), we are adopted (we are a part of God's family and belong), and we are confident (we live by what we know and believe).

CHAPTER 5

TELLING ANGER GOODBYE

Everyone experiences anger. It is the earliest emotion to have, and it is the laziest emotion to have. It takes no discipline. It is available to anyone, anywhere, at any time. You can experience it at the store when someone breaks in line in front of you, when a fellow driver cuts you off in traffic, when the outcome of an event didn't turn out like you wanted it to, or when you didn't get the response from a person you wanted. Anger can happen quickly without warning. It can change your day from good to bad, your attitude from positive to negative, and your mood from happy to sad.

Anger can come from unresolved issues, such as abuse, betrayal, disappointment, family problems, financial concerns, health needs, injustice, loss, marriage challenges, mistreatment, offenses, stress, rejection, or being violated.

Anger can become a problem when we have trouble controlling it, causing us to say or do things we later regret. Uncontrolled anger can quickly escalate to verbal abuse and physical violence. Irritation - no matter how small - can cause an angry person to blow up, lose their cool, or set them off. Anger is often a cover for fear, hurt, sadness, and shame. Unresolved anger can lead to anxiety, depression, and other health issues. Anger management and therapy are common issues in relationship counseling.

There are four stages to unresolved anger. First, there is what I call the build-up.

Unresolved or repressed anger builds up over time. A person may not know how to express anger. When this occurs, it becomes bigger and bigger, much like continuing to blow up a balloon.

Next is what I refer to as the bring-on. This is what ignites, provokes, or sparks anger. Triggers, like events, memories, people, and places, can set it off.

Third in my list, is the blow-up. This is when we start using hurtful words. It's like pouring gasoline on a fire. This sort of aggression most always leads to harm.

Finally, is the backlash. Now the consequences come into play and lead to regret and remorse.

In the Book of Proverbs, Solomon wrote about unresolved anger. Here are some of his quotes.

Proverbs 14:17 - "A quick-tempered man acts foolishly."

Proverbs 14:29 - "If you stay calm, you are wise, but if you have a hot temper, you only show how stupid you are."

Proverbs 15:18 - "An angry man stirs up discord, but one slow to anger calms strife."

Proverbs 16:32 - "He who is slow to anger is better than the mighty."

Proverbs 19:19 - "If someone has a hot temper, let him take the consequences. If you get him out of trouble once, you will have to do it again."

Proverbs 29:11 - "A fool gives full vent to anger, but a wise person quietly holds it back."

Solomon even warned against keeping company with angry people in Proverbs 22:24-25, "Make no friendship with an angry man, and with a furious man do not go, lest you learn his ways and set a snare for your soul."

Not all anger is evil. There is such a thing as legitimate anger. It is sometimes called righteous indignation. There are times when a person has every right to be angry. When someone has been unnecessarily offended, it is just for them to express their anger. The violated person has the right to pursue justice through society's proper and lawful means to correct an injustice and hold guilty people accountable for their evil deeds. This is controlled anger. Uncontrolled anger is destructive and causes much harm. On the other hand, controlled anger can be constructive by correcting an injustice or bringing restitution where possible.

Controlled anger uses energy and resources to bring good out of a bad situation. Jesus set a great example of this when He entered the Jewish Temple of Worship and found it had been turned into a marketplace (John 2:13-16). People were using the Temple to make money for personal gain. Jesus became so angry that He made a whip, overturned tables, and drove the marketeers and animals out of the Temple, restoring its original purpose. Jesus was angry at how He found the Temple and used His energy to make things right. He discovered something negative and changed it to be positive through his anger.

Controlling anger was an issue the Apostle Paul gave instructions for in Ephesians 4:26-27, "Don't sin by letting anger gain control over you. Don't let the sun go down while you are still angry, for anger gives a mighty foothold to the Devil."

Paul's teaching is clear; it is not a sin to be angry, but it is a sin to let your anger get out of control. Uncontrolled anger is destructive and dangerous because it gives Satan a foothold in your life. The Devil is always looking for an opportunity to take advantage of you. Remaining angry is a destructive tool that he uses. Remember, Jesus identified him as a thief who comes to steal, kill, and destroy (John 10:10).

Paul didn't give us unrealistic instruction that suggests we should never become angry. Instead, his teaching is practical and helpful. It is going to happen! The goal is not that we should never become angry. Instead, we must learn how to deal with anger and bring it under control. No one wants to be controlled by anger. Solomon warned us of uncontrolled anger in Proverbs 25:28, "A person without self-control is like a city with broken-down walls." Every Old Testament city had walls for defense and protection. A City whose walls were broken down could no longer defend or protect itself. The inability to defend meant their enemies could attack them anytime and from any direction. The same thing is true of a person with uncontrolled anger. That is a dangerous way to live. Here are seven tips about controlling anger that the Lord has helped me to see.

LET GOD HELP YOU

God is our helper. The one who created you knows how to help you. David said in Psalm 46:1, " God is our refuge and strength, always ready to help in times of trouble." God helps us in many ways. Let's look at just a few of them.

Prayer - Psalm 120:1, "I took my troubles to the Lord; I cried out to Him, and He answered my prayer." Prayer isn't based on rituals, traditions, or theological terminology. Prayer that prevails comes from the heart. Cry out to God from your heart, and ask Him to help you with your anger. The Word of God is spiritual food. Our physical body needs food to function, and so does our spirit. 1 Timothy 4:6, Paul taught that we are nourished by words of faith that help us grow, develop, and become stronger. That's why we need a healthy balanced diet of the Word of God.

The Holy Spirit - In Galatians 5:19-23, Paul shows the differences between "the works of the flesh" and "the fruit of the Spirit." Notice that our flesh is known by its work, while the Holy Spirit produces fruit. One of the works of the flesh is anger (verse 20). However, the fruit of the Spirit includes temperance or self-control (verse 23). The Holy Spirit can even help you control destructive outbursts of anger.

IDENTIFY THE SOURCE

Know the source of your anger and get to the root of it. What is causing it? Is there a particular person or group that triggers your anger? Where is it coming from? Is it from abuse in the past that you've never dealt with? Is it from a failure that you never took responsibility for? Is it from a wound that can't heal because you won't forgive? Are you the source of your anger? Ask yourself some hard questions, and be honest in answering them. Knowing the origin of your anger is vital if you want to experience victory. Be transparent like David was in Psalm 138:23-24 when he prayed, "Search me, O God, and know my heart; test me and know my anxious thoughts. Point out anything in me that offend you, and lead me along the path of everlasting life."

AVOID THE TRIGGERS

Keep a safe distance from the places, the people, and the situations that might trigger painful memories and cause you to lose control. Forgiveness doesn't mean you should be around or hang out with someone who transgressed against you. There are times when that would not be wise. Use wisdom, and know when it is time to avoid a situation. Romans 12:18 states, "If it is possible, as far as it depends on you, live at peace with everyone." Sometimes the best way to live in peace is through distance! Stay away from anyone, any place, or anything that could cause you grief. Focus on a new future, new friends, and new opportunities!

TAKE A TIMEOUT

When two basketball teams are feeling the heat of competition, it is common for one of the coaches to call a time-out. A 60-second break can make the difference for a struggling team to regain composure. A person can become so angry that their judgment is impaired. That's the time to call a time-out. If you have ever experienced a panic attack, you know how frightening it can feel. If left untreated, it can lead to an emotional meltdown. Taking time out to step away can cause such feelings to settle down. By doing this, you are taking control of your response. It's the perfect time to pray and think about what is happening so that you can redirect your thoughts and make good decisions. It's also helpful to talk to yourself. Listen to how David talked to himself in Psalm 42:11, "Why, my soul, are you downcast? Why so disturbed within me? Put your Hope in God!" Take a break, and tell yourself, My hope is in God, and I'm in control of my emotions! I may not be able to control what happened to me in the past, but I can make good choices. I am in control of my thoughts, emotions, and behavior. Anger is not in control of me. The past is not in control of me. People who hurt me are not in control of me. I am in control of myself!

STOP FUELING IT

In Proverbs 26:20, Solomon gives us the answer to stopping the problem of gossip. Stop fueling it! He said, "Where there is no wood, the fire goes out; and where there is no talebearer, strife ceases." If you stop putting wood on a fire, it will go out. This is true with gossip and anger. If you want anger to die, you've got to stop fueling it. There will come a time you must stop talking about your offense, or anger will never die. By continually talking about your pain, you are keeping anger alive. Only discuss your situation with trusted family, friends, or counselors. At the beginning of your recovery, you may need to talk often. However, as you go through the stages of emotional healing, the need to discuss your situation will gradually lessen. Then, as you reach wholeness from your wound, the day will come you won't need to talk about it anymore. Some people never heal from the past because they never stop talking about it. Once you've buried it, don't dig it back up by talking about it! There might be an occasion when you need someone to talk

WORK ON YOURSELF

Winston Churchill said, "Never let a good crisis go to waste." Whatever caused your anger can be used for good. Something good can come out of it. So don't waste the opportunity to bring good things out of bad experiences. Use that energy to work on yourself. Anger can be a great motivator if you let it drive you in the right direction.

This principle also has a spiritual application. Whatever your dealing with can draw you closer to God, or away from God. You will decide which direction it takes you. James 4:8 "Come close to God, and God will come close to you. I love the simplicity of this scripture. We come close to God through prayer, worship, and His Word (reading, studying, meditating), and as we come close to Him, He comes close to us!

This also applies emotionally. Emotional work can be challenging because we sometimes find ourselves to be unstable in our thinking. James 1:8 describes an emotionally unstable person as, "a double-minded man who is unstable in all his ways." Doubled-minded means two minds, hearts, and souls which will always lead to divided loyalties and allegiances. James describes this person as a wave of the sea, blown and tossed by the wind. This means the direction of their lives is determined by circumstances and situations. They are easily confused, influenced, and deceived because they are not emotionally stable. This is not the person you want to be! David describes emotionally stable people in Psalm 1:3 as "trees planted along the riverbanks bearing fruit each season. Their leaves never wither, and they prosper in all they do." Emotionally unstable people are blown about and tossed while emotionally stable people are planted and productive!

Believe it or not, staying in shape physically makes a big difference in our spiritual and emotional well-being. 1 Corinthians 6:19-20 reminds us that our body is the Temple of the Holy Spirit. Take care of the Temple! Here are just a few tips from everybody's list for healthy Living:

- Eat Right (Balanced and healthy diet)
- Sleep Good (Eight hours)
- Exercise (Get up and move)
- Hydrate (Drink water)
- Rest (Chill out)

TELL IT GOODBYE

Anger produces so many negative effects. Anger causes serious health issues. Unchecked anger usually leads to relationship problems, robbing you of joy, energy, peace, and contentment. Anger will keep you from living your best life. Don't wait until anger has taken so much from you before you deal with it. Dealing with anger isn't feeding it, nursing it, or justifying it. The best way I know to deal with anger is to make up your mind that you will not live the rest of your life defenseless, like a city whose walls are broken down. Having no defense permits the enemy to use anger against us in all sorts of ways. However, God wants to help you rebuild the walls of your life by observing the important principles we have discussed. First, identify the source of your anger. Next, avoid the situations and people that trigger your anger. Another is to take a timeout when you feel things spiraling out of control. Refuse to fuel the anger, work on yourself, and tell anger goodbye!

Psalm 37:8 reminds us to "Stop being angry! Turn from your rage! Do not lose your temper-it only leads to harm." Ephesians 4:31 "Get rid of all bitterness, rage, anger, harsh words, and slander, as well as all types of evil behavior." Colossians 3:8

"Now is the time to get rid of anger, rage, malicious behavior, slander, and dirty language."

CHAPTER 6

FACTS ABOUT FORGIVENESS

From 1951 - 59, NBC Television aired a very popular police drama television program named, Dragnet. Then in 1967 - 70, they decided to bring it back for four more seasons. The crime-solving mysteries were led by Sergeant Joe Friday, and his partners, Officer Frank Smith, and Officer Bill Cannon. Sergeant Friday and his partners were dedicated police detectives who would methodically investigate crimes in Los Angeles, California. One of its trademarks was the show's opening narration: "Ladies and gentlemen, the story you are about to hear is true. Only the names have been changed to protect the innocent." Sergeant Friday was a no-nonsense kind of guy. He would often say, "Just the facts please," when questioning a witness, or someone who knew a person involved in breaking the law. Friday knew the difference between details and facts. People often get bogged down in details that can be irrelevant and even confusing at times. Learning the facts can bring clarity and closure to a case. Sargent Friday knew discovering the facts was critical to helping him find the answers he needed in solving a crime.

God's forgiveness is life's greatest experience. Nothing compares to it. After ministering on forgiveness one Sunday morning, a gentleman came to me and said, "That was a really good Baptist sermon!" My response was, "Forgiveness is not a Baptist thing, Methodist thing, Catholic thing, or Pentecostal thing. Forgiveness is a God thing." The reason God's forgiveness is so powerful is it releases us from our sins and is the first step in having a righteous relationship with God, our Father.

In Luke 10:17-20, Jesus' disciples excitedly came to Him declaring that they had discovered spiritual authority over demonic spirits through his name. Jesus' response most likely surprised them when He said, "Don't celebrate because you have power over demons, but celebrate because your names are registered as citizens of heaven." Jesus needed to use this important revelation to teach the priority of forgiveness. You and I are citizens of the city, county, state, and nation where we live. Yet, we are also citizens of Heaven, God's eternal world to come, because of God's forgiveness.

King David experienced God's forgiveness and wrote about it in Psalm 32 and Psalm 51. Most Christians are well aware that David sinned horribly when he committed adultery with Bathsheba and had her husband, Uriah, murdered on the front line of battle. Some Bible scholars believe David went about a year before confessing his sin. Only when the Lord sent the prophet Nathan (2 Samuel 12) to confront David with his evil deeds did he confess his sin. Unconfessed sin causes devastating results. Proverbs 28:13 says, "He who covers his sins will not prosper, but whoever confesses and forsakes them will have mercy." David's unconfessed sin took a toll on him physically and mentally. Psalm 32:3 and 51:3 are partial records of David's regret. He said, "When I refused to confess my sin, I was weak and miserable, and I groaned all day long...For I recognize my shameful deeds—they haunt me day and night." Of course, there were spiritual ramifications. Psalm 51:10 records his famous prayer of contrition, "Create in me a clean heart, O God. Renew a right spirit within me."

In response to David's plea for forgiveness, God did what God always does, He forgave him; "Oh, what joy for those whose rebellion is forgiven, whose sin is put out of sight! Yes, what joy for those whose record the Lord has cleared of sin, whose lives are lived in complete honesty" Psalm 32:1-2. Then, in Psalm 103:12, "As far as the east is from the west, so far has he removed our transgressions from us." The phrase "as far as the east is from the west" speaks of infinite space. This is different from the north and south. You can travel north only so far and then you will be forced to travel south. It is 12,430 miles from the North Pole to the South Pole. North and south meet at poles, but east and west never meet. You can board a flight going east and fly eastward around the world. As long as you are going east, you'll never get to the west. If you're flying west, you'll never get to the east. If David had said, as far as the north is from the south so far has he removed our transgressions that would have meant God's forgiveness would have limitations. But David said east from west which means God's forgiveness is limitless. This description of God's unlimited forgiveness came from a man who had sinned against God in horrible ways, yet also knew firsthand the greatest experience in life, God's forgiveness.

As Sargent Friday in Dragnet always said, "Just the facts please," here are seven facts about forgiveness that can help you in your understanding of God's forgiveness.

FACT NUMBER ONE: EVERYONE NEEDS FORGIVENESS

The human race is made up of many different nationalities of people, and our one common denominator is that we all need forgiveness. We were all born with sin in our DNA. The Apostle Paul wrote in Romans 3:23, " For all have sinned; all fall short of God's glorious standard." The Prophet Isaiah said in Isaiah 53:6, " All of us have strayed away like sheep. We have left God's paths to follow our own." There are no perfect people born into this world. We have all missed the mark, come short of God's glory, and had times when we didn't measure up. We have all made mistakes, bad choices, and wrong decisions. We are all guilty of doing things we shouldn't have done, and saying things we shouldn't have said. The word all used by Paul and Isaiah leaves no one out. It means all of us! We all need forgiveness.

The reason we were born sinners goes back to the first man, Adam. We inherited our sinful nature from Adam due to his disobedience. Today, there is great interest in genealogy, and tracing family history and roots. Romans 5:12 traces the human race's ancestry back to the first man, "When Adam sinned, sin entered the entire human race. Adam's sin brought death, so death spread to everyone, for everyone sinned." Due to Adam's disobedience, we were all born with sin in our nature, and all possess the need for forgiveness.

FACT NUMBER TWO: FORGIVENESS IS AVAILABLE TO EVERYONE

When Joseph, Jesus' earthly father, was considering breaking off his engagement to Mary because of her unexplained pregnancy, the angel of The Lord appeared to him in a dream. He revealed that the child in Mary's womb was conceived by the Holy Spirit. Then the angel announced that the child's name was to be Jesus and that His purpose for coming into the world was to offer people forgiveness for their sins, (Matthew 1:19-21).

The Apostle Paul wrote about this good news in Romans 5:18. "Yes, Adam's one sin brings condemnation for everyone, but Christ's one act of righteousness brings a right relationship with God and new life for everyone." Paul also tells us in Titus 2:11 "The grace of God has been revealed, bringing salvation to all people."

Perhaps the most famous scripture in the Bible, John 3:16 and 17, makes it very clear that God's forgiveness is available to everyone, "For God so loved the world that he gave his only Son so that everyone who believes in him will not perish but have eternal life. God did not send his Son into the world to condemn it, but to save it." God's forgiveness is for all people, not just a few.

In 1829, George Wilson and James Porter robbed a United States mail carrier in Pennsylvania, Both men were captured and tried in a court of law. In May of 1830 they were found guilty of six charges including robbery of the mail, and putting the life of the driver in jeopardy. Wilson and Porter received the sentence of "Execution by Hanging," which was to be carried out on July 2, 1830.

George Wilson's family and friends took petitions of signatures to President Andrew Jackson asking for mercy. President Jackson issued George Wilson a pardon from execution, and his sentence was reduced from being hung to serving 20 years in prison. To everyone's amazement, George Wilson turned down the President's pardon. This decision confused the President. As a result, the United States Supreme Court issued the following ruling: "The Court cannot give the prisoner the benefit of the pardon unless he claims the benefit of it...It is a grant to him: it is his property: and he may accept it or not as he pleases." So a pardon, even though signed by the President of the United States, is only good if received by the guilty. George Wilson refused his pardon from the President of the United States and was hanged.

Christ's dying on the cross, provided your pardon from sin, but it is only good if you receive it. When it comes to God's forgiveness, you can't earn it, work for it, pay for it, or deserve it. You can only ask for it and receive it. If you are struggling with your past failures or sins, ask God for His forgiveness, and receive it. If you are having difficulty receiving God's forgiveness because of guilt or shame, remember Isaiah 55:7, "Our God will abundantly pardon."

FACT NUMBER THREE: FORGIVENESS IS A GIFT

The Apostle Paul made it clear that forgiveness is a gift from God in three scriptures: Romans 6:23, "For the wages of sin is death, but the free gift of God is eternal life through Christ Jesus our Lord;" Ephesians 2:8, "God saved you by His grace when you believed. And you can't take credit for this; it is a gift from God;" and 2 Corinthians 9:15 "Thank God for His Son-a gift too wonderful for words!" From these three scriptures, we learn:

- Forgiveness is a gift from God.
- Jesus paid for the gift of forgiveness on the cross.
- The gift of forgiveness changes our eternal destination.
- The gift of forgiveness is indescribable! Words are not adequate.

In Luke 7, Jesus and His disciples went home for a meal with a Pharisee named Simon. This was unusual because the Pharisees were some of Jesus' critics. The Pharisees were a Jewish sect who are mentioned 98 times in the New Testament. They believed a person's relationship with God was based upon how well one could keep their list of rules which consisted of 613 laws.

As Jesus and His disciples were sitting around a table in Simon's house enjoying a meal a woman walked in. Luke doesn't give us her name, but in the book of John, she is identified as Mary. Luke describes Mary as a sinner, and Jesus himself states that she had many sins. It is a common belief that Mary was a prostitute. To fully understand what was happening, you need to get a mental picture of this setting. Jesus and His disciples were having a meal with Simon, a Pharisee, when a woman named Mary, who was a sinner with many sins and believed to be a prostitute, walked into the house, uninvited. When she entered, the setting completely changed with a Pharisee on one side of the table, and a prostitute on the other side; talk about mixed company?!

Before Mary entered the house the focus was on Simon. It was Simon's house, his table, and his meal. After Mary enters the house the focus shifts to her. Simon was not happy about Mary crashing his party. Jesus began a conversation with Mary that led to a powerful statement when He said to her, "Your sins are forgiven." Jesus gave a sinful woman the gift of forgiveness. It was the greatest gift Christ could have ever given her. Here are several observations about Christ's gift of forgiveness to Mary. First, the gift of forgiveness is what Mary needed more than anything else in her life. Next, Mary could have never paid for her forgiveness, but she could receive it. If someone gives you a gift, then hands you a receipt and asks you to pay for the gift, it is no longer a gift. If you have to pay the price of the gift it ceases to be a gift. For a gift to become your possession, all you have to do is receive it. Third, the gift of forgiveness released

Mary from her past. This is what Paul meant in 2 Corinthians 5:17 when he described those in Christ as a new creation with "old things passed away'. Next, The gift of forgiveness gave Mary peace. The last words Jesus spoke to her as she was leaving Simon's house was, "Go in peace." Romans 5:1 states that when we experience Christ's forgiveness, we then have peace with God. Finally, the gift of forgiveness changed Mary's destiny. She now had a new future! Referring again to 2 Corinthians 5:17, Mary experienced that "old things passed away and all things have been made new."

Simon probably thought that if Jesus were a prophet He would have known her lifestyle. Jesus, knowing Simon's thoughts, used this opportunity to teach a Pharisee about forgiveness. He chose an illustration of a banker who made a $500.00 loan to one man, and a $50.00 loan to another man. Neither man was able to pay back his loan, so the banker forgave them both and canceled their debts. Then Jesus asked Simon, who do you suppose loved him after that? Simon said it was the one with the largest debt. Jesus agreed and said that was why when Mary came into the house of Simon she washed His feet with her tears. Simon, however, neglected to wash the feet of Jesus. In those days and places, washing someone's feet was a sign of being welcomed in a person's house. Mary washed Jesus' feet as an expression of her gratitude for the gift of forgiveness Jesus extended to her. Those who have the largest sin debt and have been forgiven of much will love the most. What a powerful revelation Jesus taught Simon the Pharisee about the greatest gift of all, the gift of God's forgiveness.

FACT NUMBER FOUR: FORGIVENESS IS TO BE RECEIVED AND RELEASED

In Matthew 18:23-35 Jesus tells a story of a King who forgave his servant of a very large debt equal to millions of dollars in today's economy. After receiving forgiveness from the King, the same servant refused to forgive a fellow servant of a much lesser debt of thousands of dollars. Upon learning of his servant's unwillingness to forgive a debt, the King reversed his forgiveness and placed his servant in debtor's prison. Jesus said that's how His Heavenly Father responds to those who have received His forgiveness but are unwilling to give forgiveness. The servant's unwillingness to forgive a fellow servant blocked him from receiving the King's forgiveness. Jesus revealed a powerful truth that if you receive the blessing of forgiveness, then you have a responsibility to give the blessing of forgiveness.

In Matthew 6:12 Jesus gave us the receive and release principle of forgiveness when teaching us to pray, "Forgive us our sins, as we forgive those who have sinned against us." Then in verses 14 -15, Jesus said, "If you forgive those who sin against you, your Heavenly Father will forgive you. But if you refuse to forgive others, your Father will not forgive your sins." The receive and release principle of forgiveness can bring life to dead relationships, and marriages.

Sinners receive forgiveness through repentance. Repentance means an about-face or a completely turning your back on sin. Turning away from sin means walking in a new direction with Christ. Christians receive forgiveness through confession. The Apostle John reassures us that if we confess our sins, God is faithful to forgive us of our sins, (1 John 1:9). The word confess means to agree. When we confess our sins we are agreeing with God that we were wrong. When we come into agreement with God concerning our sin He is faithful to forgive us. Forgiveness is not just a one-time experience. That's why Jesus taught us to pray for continual forgiveness, and as we continually receive forgiveness, we are to continually forgive others, (Matthew 6:12).

The Dead Sea sits on the border of Israel and Jordan. It is a lake that is 42 miles long and 11 miles wide at its widest point. Also known as the Salt Sea, it is nearly 10 times as salty as the world's oceans. The Jordan River is its major source of water. The Jordan River begins at Mount Herman and flows north to south for roughly 223 miles going through the Sea of Galilee onto the Dead Sea. The Dead Sea has the lowest elevation on Earth. It contains no fish, plants, or any other visible life because it only receives and never gives. The Jordan River flows into it, but the water never flows out of it. For water to produce life it has to flow. When water just sits it loses its ability to produce life.

If we only receive forgiveness and never release forgiveness we become like stagnant water. Stagnation occurs when water stops flowing. Stagnant bodies of water are dangerous because they provide a breeding ground for insects such as mosquitoes that can transmit diseases. Only receiving and never giving means we are not healthy, and its negative effect can be carried into once-productive relationships. So we need the flow of forgiveness in our lives to be complete and whole. Ephesians 4:32 encourages us to "Be kind and compassionate to one another, forgiving each other, just as in Christ God forgave you."

Here are seven principles to remember when offering forgiveness and releasing the debtor. First, releasing is a choice. You choose to release someone of an offense. Just as Jesus choose to lay his life down on the cross (John 10:17-18) you choose to forgive. You could choose revenge. You could allow getting even, or settling the score be your motive. Yet, you take the high road and choose to release and let it go. Choices are powerful and determine our future. You make a great investment into your future by releasing.

Next, releasing is a major step in emotional healing. In dealing with an offense you can experience a wide range of emotions. Emotions such as anger, bitterness, and resentment will keep you from achieving emotional wholeness. Until you release the offense it will continue to torment you. This torment can go on for years after the offense was committed. The best way to defuse negative emotions that are hindering your well-being is to release them. Just keep letting it go!

Third, releasing breaks the burden of the past. The longer you carry the past the heavier it gets. Your past will wear you out if you continue to carry it. The weight of yesterday's negative circumstances will rob you of the joy you can experience today. That's why it is emotionally unhealthy to live in the past. People who live in the past stay defeated. Don't let your past be an emotional resident in your heart, or a mental resident in your mind. Breaking the heaviness of your past off your life always begins with releasing it.

Fourth, releasing will make you stronger as a person. Yes, it will stretch you, but it will not kill you. As Kelly Clarkson sings, What doesn't kill you makes you stronger. Forgiveness stretches you so that you become a better and stronger you. Bodybuilders know the key to their success is stretching muscles by lifting weights. Pumping iron means resistance. It is the resistance that develops muscles. In releasing you may encounter resistance. The resistance can come from a flashback, an event, or something that was said, but you just keep releasing it even if it hurts. This is the resistance that is building character in you, and making you stronger.

Number five, releasing is not based on being worthy. You will rarely forgive someone who deserves it. Jesus didn't forgive the thief on the cross who cried out to him because he was worthy. The man was a thief who deserved his punishment of crucifixion. Jesus forgave him because that was His purpose for coming to the world.

I Timothy 1:15 says, "Christ Jesus came into the world to save (forgive) sinners." Offering forgiveness to people who don't deserve it is exactly what Jesus did and still does today.

Six, releasing is setting an awesome example for others to follow. You are never more like Jesus than when you forgive. Your release may be the only positive example some people may ever see of what forgiveness is. So ask yourself, what kind of example do I want to set? Extending forgiveness can be a powerful part of your witness for Christ.

Finally, releasing brings the blessings of God into your life. By forgiving, you remove all the hindrances. Hindrances that have been blocking God's blessings from your life. Blessings such as healing, freedom, and joy. Releasing opens the door to God's blessings while carrying a grudge closes the door to his blessings. Offering forgiveness today can bring great blessings upon your tomorrow.

FACT NUMBER FIVE: FORGIVENESS IS A PROCESS

The process is a series of actions taken to achieve a particular goal. Every action taken is done with the goal in mind. Simon Peter asked Jesus, " How often should I forgive someone who sinned against me? Seven times?" (Matthew 18:21-22). In Jewish teachings, a person was required to forgive someone up to three times for an offense. Once you had forgiven three times, that was it. So when Peter brought up the forgiveness issue and used the number seven it sounded spiritual. The number seven means completion. It seemed that Peter had mastered forgiveness by more than doubling the required times of forgiving someone of an offense. I'm sure Peter was not ready for Jesus' response to his question. My interpretation of how Jesus responded to Peter goes like this, "Wrong! You are not even close. How about seven times seventy!" Imagine Peter trying to wrap his mind around 490 times a day. The reason Peter's understanding of forgiveness had to do with a number was because he had it in his head, but not his heart. Forgiveness has to do with both your head and heart. Jesus was teaching Peter that forgiveness is not about numbers, but continually extending grace to someone who has trespassed against you until you have reached the goal of forgiveness.

God's forgiveness is available to us the moment we confess our sins and ask for forgiveness. When the thief cried out

Jesus responded immediately reassuring him of his forgiveness by stating that he would be with Christ in paradise that day. However, it is completely different with people because of what offenses do to us emotionally, mentally, and spiritually. When dealing with offenses it is important to remember that forgiveness is a process and not a one-time event. This process can be extremely painful and difficult because of memories, emotions, and wounds. The truth is forgiveness is not a natural act. That's why we struggle with it. The natural man says an eye for an eye. You hurt me, I'll hurt you. In the natural revenge is always the goal. So to go through the process of forgiveness you have to go to a new level of thinking and living spiritually. When you forgive It forces you to change. Forgiveness will make you grow up. You will have to put away childish things (1 Corinthians 13:11), or you'll never reach the goal of forgiveness. Here are some important steps in the process of reaching your goal of forgiveness.

1. Acknowledge It. Living in denial is never healthy. Coming to a place where you acknowledge what happened can be extremely painful, but it is a first step in your recovery. Sometimes you just can't believe it happened to you, and that you are where you are in life. I've heard people say I never dreamed I would be at this place in my life. This is called shock. The shock of what happened means it is taking time for you to absorb it. It was just too much to comprehend all at one time. So with time to process it, you will be able to acknowledge it.

2. Accept It. You can't change what happened. It's not what you wanted or asked for, but it happened. Now accepting it is another big step moving forward. The most painful things in life are the things you can't change. Paul wrote about this in 2 Corinthians 12:7-9 and identified it as a thorn in the flesh. A thorn represents pain. If you have ever had a thorn piercing your skin you know pain. Paul prayed three times for God to remove it, and nothing changed. The thorn and the pain remained with him. Then Paul learns about God's grace. God reassures Paul by

saying, "My grace is sufficient for you. My strength is perfected in your weakness." Grace is God's favor, yet it is more than that. Grace is also God giving me the ability to deal with the painful things in life I can't change.

3. Admit It. It is okay to admit your struggles. Don't compare yourself to someone else who may have gone through a similar situation, and by all appearances is doing good. Where you are in your healing, and where someone else is in your healing can be two different places. Just because you are struggling now doesn't mean you will always struggle. The path to recovery will always include a struggle. There is always a struggle before a victory. The struggle often feels like you've made one step forward and two steps backward. In the Bible, every great person of faith had their struggle. Even Jesus struggled in the Garden of Gethsemane. You may not see it or feel it, but it's often in the struggle that you are getting stronger and stronger. God often uses our struggles as preparation for our future.

4, Allow It. Grieving the past is painful. There are no shortcuts or by-passes. There are no easy cures or quick fixes. You need to experience every part of grief to completely heal. Someone said when we are grieving we need the three Ts: Talk, Tears, and Time. Find someone who is confidential that you can talk to. Often this will be someone other than a family member. Cry when you need to. Don't rush your healing. Time is a very important element of healing. Allow the healing to happen. I remember as a child scraping my arm or leg while playing. As a scab would develop over the wound I would pick at it and remove it. My mother would say, stop picking at it so it can heal. There comes a time when the best thing you can do is leave a wound alone so that it can heal.

5. Ask For It. The process of forgiveness has its challenges. It can be extremely difficult at times. Ask the Lord to help you in the process. In Psalm 61, David is overwhelmed at life and cries out to God saying, "Lead me to the rock that is

higher than me." David calls God a rock. Israel is a very rocky land with huge rocks making up mountains. A rock represents strength and stability. If you're struggling with forgiveness, go to the rock, God, and ask him to help you. Remember what Jesus had to say about asking in Matthew 7:7-8 (NIV) "Ask, and it will be given you; seek, and you will find; knock, and the door will be opened to you. For everyone who asks receives; the one who seeks finds; and the one who knocks, the door will be opened."

6. Agree With It. Come into agreement with God's Word. Don't play the victim. Don't let a failure or defeat define you. Jeremiah 17:14 "Heal me Lord, and I will be healed." Make up your mind that you will not live wounded for the rest of your life. With God, the rest of your life can be the best of your life! This doesn't mean your world will return to the way it was, but it does mean you as a person will be healed so that you can move forward with your life. Agree with Isaiah 54:17 "No weapon formed against you shall prosper." Agree with Romans 8:37 that you are "more than a conqueror." Agree with 1 John 5:4 "I am born of God, and overcome the world, and this is the victory that overcomes the world, even our faith."

7. Affirm It Proverbs 18:21 teaches us death and life are in the power of the tongue. So speak life over yourself and confess the following:

- I am in the process of forgiveness.
- The offense against me will not destroy me.
- I release everyone who transgressed against me.
- God is my strength, and through Him I am strong.
- I am a victor, not a victim, and overcome all hurts.
- I believe God is working all things for my good.
- I have a bright future because God has plans to bless and prosper me.

Affirmation is very important. Affirm your future by speaking life and victory. Revelation 12:11 teaches us to overcome our enemy, Satan, by the blood of the Lamb (Jesus), and word of our testimony.

FACT NUMBER SIX: FORGIVENESS IS NOT WHAT YOU MAY THINK

There are many misconceptions about forgiveness. Unfortunately, many in the Christian community are uneducated about the powerful truths concerning forgiveness. Forgiveness is not just playing the grace card when someone is caught in sin. Grace is not permission to sin, and then not being held accountable for one's actions. It is very important to know and understand what forgiveness is and what forgiveness is not.

Forgiveness is not approval or agreement Just because you forgive someone doesn't mean you approve or agree with the offense. In John chapter eight Jesus forgave a woman caught in adultery. While Jesus extended forgiveness to her, he didn't approve of her behavior or justify her actions by agreeing with her. Jesus instructed her to go and sin no more. He is instructing her to change her lifestyle. Jesus did not enable her to continue as she was by approving of her sin but empowered the woman to change by forgiving her and correcting her.

Forgiveness is not Minimizing The Offense. It doesn't mean the offense didn't happen, or what was done to you is okay. Neither does it mean the brokenness and pain you experienced weren't real, or The person who hurt you is welcome back in your life. It doesn't mean that trust or respect will be restored, or that reconnection is possible. It doesn't even mean you will ever forget the offense.

It's important to understand that an offense is not just a difference of opinion. It is a transgression against another person. It is a serious sin that should never be taken lightly. Minimizing an offense only compounds a bad situation by leaving an offended person feeling confused, and full of self-doubt. To invalidate or belittle someone's painful experience is a lack of compassion and a form of emotional abuse.

Forgiveness does not mean instant emotional healing. First of all, instant emotional healing is not a thing. So just because there has been forgiveness does not imply that the person who was offended is suddenly all better. You can forgive and still hurt. You can forgive and still be wounded. Forgiveness is one step you take toward emotional healing, but it is not the only step. Emotional healing takes time. Sometimes it takes years. This is where people can be very insensitive when making statements like, you need to get over it or you need to move on. I had both said to me. Can you imagine walking into an Intensive Care Unit at a hospital to visit a friend who is very sick, struggling to breathe, and saying, you need to get over this or why don't you get well? When people make insensitive comments about your recovery you have to understand if they have never been where you are in life they don't understand. Just as the old song, Walk A Mile In My Shoes, says, "Before you abuse, criticize, and accuse. Then walk a mile in my shoes."

Forgiveness does not mean there are no consequences. There are times when we think that forgiveness erases consequences but that is not to be assumed. Forgiveness and consequences are two completely different things. The offended person might forgive but there might be penalties to pay or laws that have been broken.

David knew firsthand the incredible joy of experiencing God's forgiveness. Psalm 32:1 "Oh, what joy for those whose sin is forgiven." However, the forgiveness of his sins did not take away the consequences of his sins. Galatians 6:7 teaches us that we will always reap what we sow. You can reap the consequences of sin even after the forgiveness of sin, even years later.

The Prophet Nathan told King David there would be consequences to his actions: If you will remember, Nathan prophesied to David that because of his blatant sin and disregard for others, the sword would be a constant threat to his family (2 Samuel 12:10). The sword represents conflict. David's family would be in conflict, and become dysfunctional from that day forward.

He also said that David's sin would be publicly exposed (2 Samuel 12:12). David committed his sins privately, but the disgrace of his sins would be public for all of Israel to see.

Then he told the King that his sins had given the Lord's enemies a great opportunity to despise and blaspheme Him (2 Samuel 12:14). David had opened a door for the enemies of the Lord to do much damage to Israel.

There were further consequences of David's sin. The baby that David and Bathsheba conceived became sick and died. Even after David prayed and fasted for a week, the child died (2 Samuel 12:15-23). David's son, Amnon, raped his sister, Tamar (2 Samuel 13:1-20). David's son, Absalom, murdered his brother, Amnon (2 Samuel 13:21-39). Next, Absalom led a rebellion against David to overthrow him and seize his power as King of Israel, but Absalom died in battle (2 Samuel 15-18). However, before he died, Absalom, betrayed and insulted his father King David by having sex with ten of his wives and concubines "in the sight of all Israel," (2 Samuel 15:16, 16:21-22).

Forgiveness is not a sign of weakness It takes a strong person to forgive. You grow stronger every time you choose to forgive, love unconditionally, release a debt and let it go, pardon someone who doesn't deserve it, forgive someone who doesn't ask for it, turn the other cheek, decide not to respond to evil with evil, do good to someone who hurt you, resist speaking critical of someone who did you wrong, or bless those who have cursed you.

As you grow stronger you will be able to disregard dates, memories, events, and emotions that once had negative effects on you, and caused you a great deal of anguish. You can do this because you are growing stronger!

FACT NUMBER SEVEN: FORGIVENESS IS FREEDOM

The Greek word for forgive is aphiemi, and it means to release. To release is to set free, to let go, to cancel, or to discharge. It is the picture of totally freeing and releasing someone from a transgression or crime. An example of this is the President of the United States of America pardoning a prisoner for a crime which results in being released from prison. It means a person who was found guilty by a jury, and sentenced by a judge is now released from the crime and punishment by the President. Being set free from imprisonment may not seem fair to some, but it is possible because of being pardoned. This new freedom gives a once-convicted person a second chance in life.

Forgiveness isn't just freedom for the guilty, but it's also freedom for the person who suffered an injustice. Extending forgiveness is a major step to personal healing, and overcoming an offense. Unforgiveness will make you a hostage to the offense. Carrying a grudge will make you a prisoner of the past. When you forgive someone you are setting yourself free from the offense. Forgiveness frees you to laugh again, love again, and live again.

Forgiveness breaks the chains of anger, bitterness, and resentment that will keep you tied to an offense. It is extremely difficult to overcome an offense as long as you have emotional ties to it. Through forgiveness, you break all unhealthy connections to the past and are free to move forward into your new future. Enjoy your new freedom!

CHAPTER 7

THE ROAD TO RECOVERY

The road to recovery can be a long one with delays, detours, and dead ends. This road will take you through unfamiliar territory you didn't even know existed. It will cause you to examine your priorities, and live by a belief system based upon what is important in life. If you let it, the road to recovery will develop a better you, a more compassionate you, and a stronger you.

When I speak of recovery, I mean that it is the returning to a normal state, or developing a new normal state. Recovery is a part of life. We see it every day. It could be a person recovering from surgery, or treatments such as chemo or radiation, an athlete recovering from a sports injury, a man recovering from an automobile accident, someone recovering from an addiction to drugs or alcoholism, a woman in divorce recovery, a major corporation recovering from financial setbacks, a country or city recovering from a natural disaster such as an earthquake or hurricane. Recovery is always happening.

In Luke 15, Jesus taught a great lesson on recovery by using three illustrations: A shepherd who left his flock of ninety-nine to recover the one sheep who had wandered off so that his flock would be complete; A woman who cleaned her house diligently until she recovered a valuable coin; and a son who returned home and recovered from some terrible choices he had made. Jesus' lesson on recovery teaches us several important truths.

It doesn't take much living to learn that loss is a part of life. There may be many reasons for losing something or someone. In the stories of Jesus, it was a sheep that wandered off from the flock, a woman who misplaced a coin, and a son making bad decisions.

He also shows us that recovery is always possible. In all three of the stories Jesus told, what had been lost, was recovered. The shepherd recovered his sheep, the woman recovered her coin, and the son recovered from his poor choices. Recovery means there is hope even for the worst of our choices. Jesus taught that all things are possible for the person who believes (Mark 9:23).

Understanding that recovery takes effort is very important. It requires work and discipline to regain what was lost. The shepherd had to leave his flock and go searching for his one lost sheep. The woman had to get her broom and sweep the house until she found her coin. The son had to come to his senses and pick himself up out of terrible circumstances to return home. You have to want it, or as we commonly hear, "You have to be in it to win it." You have to be committed and be in it for the long haul until the recovery is completed.

Recovery needs to be celebrated. In each one of the brief stories that Jesus told in Luke chapter fifteen, there was a celebration when the lost thing was recovered. The shepherd, the woman, and the father each threw a party and invited family and friends to join in the celebration of their recovery. Recovery should always be celebrated!

Recovery is a part of every great testimony, success story, and victory in life. To everyone who has experienced a major setback, and made a comeback - Celebrate! To everyone who got knocked down, and got back up to try again - Celebrate! To everyone who suffered defeat and rebounded to win - Celebrate!

RECOVERY IS NOT JUST WHAT CAN BE SEEN ON THE OUTSIDE

Inside of a person is where recovery begins. The Luke 15 parable of the son returning home to his father's embrace and celebration, is an amazing story of recovery. The party is where the story ended, but where did the recovery begin? It began in verse 17, "When he came to his senses, he said, How many of my father's hired servants have food to spare, and here I am starving to death?" The son's recovery began on the inside when he began to think and reason. Then the recovery manifested itself on the outside in verse 18, "I will set out and go back to my father and say to him: 'Father, I have sinned against heaven and you.'" The son's recovery began on the inside, and then we see it on the outside when he goes back home to his father.

The prophet Isaiah gives a powerful description of how Jesus would bring recovery from sin 700 years before the birth of Christ. In Isaiah chapter 53, he describes the crucifixion of Jesus with four words. First, he was oppressed. The word oppressed in the Old Testament was used as to what taskmasters would do to make the life of a slave as miserable as possible. Then, he was afflicted which meant being treated cruelly or harshly. Next, was the word slaughter. Jesus would be like a lamb led to the slaughterhouse. Animals being slaughtered is a gruesome sight. Crucifixion was so brutal that Isaiah compared it to animals being slaughtered. The last word is sheared. Shearing was the cutting off of sheep's wool. Jesus would be sheared or stripped of everything. Not just his clothing, but his honor, respect, and dignity. The execution of Jesus was capital punishment at its worst. Isaiah also speaks of Jesus' response to such unethical treatment" in two simple, yet powerful statements: "He opened not His mouth," and, "He spoke not a word." Jesus responded with silence. He offered no resistance by verbally defending himself, declaring loudly his innocence, or complaining about the injustice of what was happening. In all four gospels: Matthew 26-27, Mark 14-15, Luke 22-23, and John 18-19, the crucifixion of Jesus played out just as Isaiah prophesied it would.

In verse 5 Isaiah spoke of the purpose of Jesus' horrible death and suffering, "He was wounded for our transgressions, He was bruised for our iniquities." The word "wounded" refers to outward bleeding. During the crucifixion, Jesus bled from seven places on His body. At the whipping post, Jesus received 39 strips on His back. The type of whip that was used had pieces of sharp rocks and metal sowed in so that it ripped flesh from His back. Blood poured from His head when a crown of thorns was pushed down into His skull. He was nailed to a cross with spikes through both hands and feet. A Roman soldier pierced His side with a spear ripping it open. Jesus was a bloody mess hanging on the cross.

Isaiah tells us the purpose for His bleeding was for our transgressions. Transgressions are sins people commit outwardly such as acts of violence, stealing, murder, adultery, etc. Jesus was wounded for the sinful behavior and physical acts of sin committed by people. The law required the shedding of an innocent animal's blood as a sacrifice for a person's sin (Hebrews 9:22). Peter confirmed Isaiah's prophecy many years later when he wrote, "God paid a ransom to save you from the empty life you inherited from your ancestors. And the ransom He paid was not mere gold or silver. He paid for you with the precious lifeblood of Christ, the sinless, spotless Lamb of God." (1 Peter 1:18-19)

Isaiah also said that Jesus would be "bruised for our iniquities." A bruise is inward bleeding. If you have a physical injury and have a bruise on your body it means there is bleeding on the inside under the skin. On the cross, Jesus bled outwardly for our outside (physical) transgressions, and He also bled inwardly for our inside (emotional and spiritual) iniquities.

Iniquities are the inside stuff that causes us great difficulties in life. Inside stuff can include anger, hatred, lack of forgiveness, bitterness, resentment, offenses, hurts, fears, and lust. It is the inside stuff that can lead to your greatest battles in life. If the inside stuff isn't dealt with it will eventually manifest itself outwardly. This is seen in a different context when Jesus said in Matthew 5:28, "Whoever looks at a woman to lust after her has already committed adultery with her in his heart." Adultery happens inwardly before it happens outwardly. Adultery takes place in a heart before it ever takes place in a bed. Solomon gave some of the greatest advice ever in Proverbs 4:23, "Above all else, guard your heart, for it affects everything you do." Solomon said to make the inside stuff (your heart) a priority because it will affect the outside stuff (your behavior).

Jesus was wounded (outward bleeding) for our transgressions, which are our physical sins. And He was bruised (inward bleeding) for our iniquities, which are our emotional sins on the cross. That's why Christ's death on the cross was so powerful. Colossians 2:13-14 reminds us, "You were dead because of your sins and because your sinful nature was not yet cut away. Then God made you alive with Christ. He forgave all our sins. He canceled the record that contained the charges against us. He took it and destroyed it by nailing it to Christ's cross."

In recovery, wholeness is the goal. Wholeness is what you need and also desire, although you might not realize it. Your wholeness may take on a new normal with all kinds of new changes, challenges, and adjustments. No one said recovery is easy. Your road to recovery will probably have some sharp curves, long and lonely stretches, and highs and lows. Recovery can involve relapses, setbacks, fears, tears, frustrations, failures, and starting over. When traveling the road to recovery, remember that it takes time.

In Mark 16:17-18, Jesus taught that one of the signs of being a believer is that a believer shall lay hands on the sick, and they recover. The word "sick" means to be in bad health or to possess a weak and broken condition. There are different types of sickness such as physical, emotional, mental, and spiritual.

The laying on of hands is simply a point of contact when praying for or with someone. It is a connection that represents agreement. In Matthew 18:19 Jesus spoke of the power of agreement in prayer, "If two of you on earth agree about anything they ask for, it will be done for them by my Father in heaven." The result of this agreement is recovery. The words "they shall" are from the Greek word "echo" which means "to have or possess." The tense used in this verse doesn't picture something instantaneous, but rather something that occurs progressively.

Likewise, the word "healed" doesn't mean instantaneous, either. Healed in Greek is "kalos" which means, "to be well, to be healthy, or to be in good shape." So the words "they shall recover" could be translated as "they shall progressively get better and better until they are healthy."

Yes, God can and does heal instantly, but in most cases, healing is progressive, especially emotional healing. There are no quick fixes or shortcuts to emotional wholeness. If you break your arm, you are going to wear a cast for about two months to protect it while the bone heals. A broken heart is far more painful than a broken arm and it takes time to heal. Don't rush it. Don't make quick decisions. Time by itself cannot heal, but time is a very important part of the healing process.

RECOVERY REQUIRES A DECISION

No one can make this decision for you. You have to take the initiative. People can pray for you, counsel you, and encourage you, but it comes down to you making a decision. In John 5:6, Jesus asked a man who had been sick for thirty-eight years, do you want to be healed? This verse has always caught my attention. Why would Jesus ask a sick man, Do you want to get well, or stay like you are? Could it have been the man had been sick so long that he had become comfortable with his sickness?

Make up your mind I will not live wounded the rest of my life. I will not play the victim. My life will not be one big pity party. After facing some very difficult times David said in Psalms 27:13 "I am confident that I will see the Lord's goodness while I am here in the land of the living." On some bad days, David decided to recover and believed he would see good days again. Decide to live again believing that good days are in your future.

Only when four leprous men sitting outside the city of Samaria made a decision did their circumstances begin to change for the better in 2 Kings 7. There came a time when they had to ask themselves the question (verse 3), "Why should we sit here waiting to die?" In grieving loss, there will come a time you will have to ask yourself some hard questions. One of them being, how long will I continue to grieve over what no longer is, or should have been? You will know when it is time to stop the grieving. Yes, you had to grieve, but remember Ecclesiastes 3:1 "To everything there is a season." Seasons are temporary. Seasons do not last forever. We have four seasons every year: winter, spring, summer, and fall. It takes all four seasons to produce balance in nature. A season lasting forever is not natural and will produce an imbalance in your life robbing you of good days. Your recovery will not happen without you making healthy decisions. Some things will not change until a decision is made. Staying in the valley of decisions creates indecisiveness which leaves you weak, and struggling. Making decisions will cause you to grow stronger. The four men made a decision, acted on it, and were greatly blessed because of it. Healthy decisions help you recover, grow stronger, and start moving toward your future.

ACCEPT WHAT YOU CAN'T CHANGE

The most painful things in life to deal with are the things you can't change or have no control over. The Apostle Paul experienced this and wrote about it in 2 Corinthians 12:7-10. Paul describes what he could not change as a thorn in the flesh. The thorn there was something like a stake that was sharp and pointed. It was used for torturing people inflicting terrible pain. Paul prayed three times asking the Lord to remove it, and nothing changed. Satan used it against Paul buffeting him. The word buffet means hitting someone with a closed fist repeatedly over and over. The thorn that caused Paul so much pain had been there for some length of time, went deep, and couldn't be removed.

What did Paul learn about the things he couldn't change? He learned about God's grace. God's grace is his unmerited love and undeserved favor. God has saving grace, and keeping grace. Through God's keeping grace we deal with things we never thought we could. We go through hardships we thought were going to destroy us. We cope with disappointments that crushed dreams and future goals.

Grace doesn't exempt you from pain. In 2 Timothy 1:11, Paul wrote about his God-given purpose of being a messenger of the gospel of Jesus Christ. In the very next verse, he wrote about the pain of being in a Roman prison. Then Paul stated that he had confidence that God would keep everything he had committed to Him. Have you ever noticed that people who do great things for God are well acquainted with pain? It seems that pain and prominence go hand in hand. The answer to what you cannot change is God's grace. Accepting the fact that your former life is over, and you will never return to it can be extremely difficult in the beginning, but God's grace is sufficient, which means it is more than enough. It takes courage to face what you didn't choose and can't change, and with God's grace, you can do it.

FIND YOUR SECRET PLACE

In Psalms 91 David talks about dwelling in the secret place of the most High and abiding under the shadow of the Almighty. David found his secret place in the presence of God, and in the presence of God, he found protection from all his enemies. Psalms 91 is all about the presence of God and the protection of God.

Jesus taught about a secret place in Matthew 6:6 and called it a closet. The Greek word for closet is tameion and means secret chamber or bedchamber. It was a place of privacy. To ensure this privacy Jesus said to close the door. Closing the door is very important because you are shutting out distractions. This verse begins with the words, "When you pray." So Jesus is teaching that prayer is about a time (when) and place (closet). Jesus is not discrediting group prayers or public praying. However, he did give a word of caution when he said if your motive in prayer is to be seen and heard by men (public recognition) you will have your fleeting reward. The closet is the place and time your relationship with your Father develops intimacy. Your closet can be anywhere. It can be an actual closet, bedroom, kitchen, laundry room, basement, or car. Jesus knew the value of a secret place. He went alone to the mountain to pray (Matthew 14:23). He went alone to the wilderness to pray (Mark 1:35). He prayed alone in the Garden of Gethsemane because he couldn't keep his disciples awake (Matthew 26:36-44). I have been blessed to stand on many platforms to preach the gospel to thousands in attendance. However, my greatest times with God were not when I was standing in front of people preaching a sermon. My greatest times with God have been in my secret place.

Jesus taught there was a time to go into the closet and a time to come out of the closet. It is in the coming out of the closet that you see God responding to your secret time with him in the closet. We pray in secret and God blesses us openly. We pray privately and God rewards us publicly. The reward doesn't come in the closet. The reward comes outside the closet so that others can see it as well. Your reward becomes a testimony of the goodness of God in full view for everyone to see. After your alone time with the Father you come out of your closet with full expectation that you will publicly see prayers answered, miracles, and blessings!

SEEK QUALIFIED CHRISTIAN COUNSELING

Don't be embarrassed about this. Of course, you don't have to advertise it. Just as you would go to a medical doctor because of a physical condition you go to a qualified trained counselor because of an emotional condition. There may be parts of your recovery that are so deep and intimate it is best not to share them with family or friends. Yet, you need someone. This is when you go for counseling in a safe and confidential setting. Ecclesiastes 4:12 "Though one may be overpowered by another, two can withstand him." The goal of counseling is to assist a person in identifying needs, discovering solutions, and developing coping skills. It is never a counselor's goal to provide the answers or make decisions for a client. These discoveries are part of a person's recovery to wholeness. How long should a person go to counseling? As long as it is needed for a person to be able to stand on their own emotions.

One of the names of Jesus is Counselor (Isaiah 9:6). Sometimes the ministry that is needed requires a private setting one on one. Not all ministry is done publicly. Christian counselors minister to broken people with wisdom and care. It is often a counselor walking a person through dark painful seasons that makes the biggest impact in a person's future. Counseling often doesn't get the credit it deserves, but it is an important ministry that has helped many people through their tough times in life.

SURROUND YOURSELF WITH TRUSTED FRIENDS

Friends are a very important connection. We all need friends. There is a big difference between a friend and an acquaintance. Be careful who you confide in. Confidentiality is a must. You don't need people you can't trust. Brake all toxic relationships. Anyone involved in betraying you, violating you, or deceiving you doesn't deserve your friendship. They will be the loser. Proverbs 17:17 "A friend loves at all times." A friend is someone loyal, genuinely concerned about you, and always speaks truth into your life. Don't try to go through recovery alone. Let a friend go with you. A friend gives you support and accountability.

POSSESS AN ATTITUDE OF GRATITUDE

Doctors tell us that it is extremely important for a patient to have a positive attitude when recovering from a sickness or surgery. Attitude affects recovery! Focus on what you have, not what you've lost. Be thankful for little blessings. Look for the good and not the bad. Believe good days are coming. Expect to see God bring blessings to you. Your attitude plays a major role in your recovery!

In Luke 17:11-19 Jesus was traveling along the border of Samaria and Galilee on his way to Jerusalem. As he enters a small village ten men with leprosy called out to Jesus from a distance. Leprosy was a chronic infectious disease that affected the skin, and nerves and would eventually lead to the rotting of flesh. There was no cure, and it was highly contagious. When the men keep their distance from Jesus they were complying with the Torah Law. Leprosy isolated you, and you never had normal relationships or friendships because of how contagious the disease was. You were known as a reject in the community which could cause a person much damage emotionally or mentally.

When the ten men called out to Jesus asking for mercy he instructed them to go show themselves to the priest, because before they could mingle with the people of the village they would have to be approved by the priest according to Leviticus 13. As they were running to the priest their leprosy disappeared. The Greek word healed in verse 15 is a primary verb that means to cure or cleanse. As they were running they were cleansed. One of the men noticed he was cleansed and went back to Jesus falling at his feet and giving thanks. Jesus asked where the other nine were. Then Jesus said to the one giving thanks, get up your faith has made you whole in verse 19. The word healed in verse 19 means well or whole. It is the Greek word, sozo, which is most commonly translated to save, rescue, or deliver. All ten men with leprosy were cleansed. Yet, the one who gave thanks was taken to a greater level of wholeness because of his attitude. A person could be cleansed from leprosy and left emotionally and mentally wounded because of all the rejection they had suffered from the disease. Yes, a person can be cleansed but not whole. The man with an attitude of gratitude was cleansed and whole. This meant he was free from all the baggage of suffering from leprosy physically, emotionally, and mentally.

CHAPTER 8

OVERCOMING OFFENSES

In Acts 24 the Apostle Paul is called before Felix, the Roman Governor, to face charges presented by Ananias, the High Priest, some Jewish leaders, and their prosecuting attorney, Tertullus. Tertullus laid out three charges against Paul when addressing the governor. The charges were as follows: First, Paul was a troublemaker who continually stirred up riots among the Jews, and lead rebellions against the Roman government. Secondly, Paul was the ringleader of a sect known as the Nazarenes who were followers of Christ from Nazareth. Thirdly, Paul taught blasphemy in the Temple defiling it with false teachings.

After Tertullus had made his presentation of charges Governor Felix allowed Paul to rise and speak. While Paul was making his self-defense case, and declaring his innocence he makes an interesting statement recorded in verse 16 "I always strive to have a conscience without offense toward God and men." The word strive means to give one's best effort like an athlete in training. Training has to do with discipline. It is extremely difficult and next to impossible to have success of any kind without discipline. An athlete will never reach his or her full potential without discipline. Military personal have to go through boot camp to be their best. A musician will need hours and hours of rehearsal to do well at a recital. Students will have to give their best to the classroom to walk on graduation day. Owning your own business will take tons of discipline. Discipline is one of the major ingredients to success in life.

One other note on the discipline of training as an athlete is that the training is done in advance. Preparation in advance is key to success. Any coach will tell you how well a ball team prepares in advance for its competition is often the difference between victory and defeat. Preparation produces confidence. Confidence produces a winning attitude. A well-prepared team takes the court or field confident they can compete against the best, and win. Preparation in advance is a top priority that sets you up for success.

When defending himself from false charges Paul said, I was prepared in advance for today, and have no offense toward God or anyone. What a powerful statement! For Paul to be able to say he was free of offenses after all the false charges against him, and all the mean acts of violence done to him (Acts 19, II Corinthians 11) was an awesome testimony. Sometimes an offense catches you off guard and does great damage to you because you weren't prepared for it. Paul is demonstrating that you can be prepared in advance for offenses so that you overcome the offense, and the offense doesn't overcome you!

Since advanced training is one of the keys to success in life let's do some advanced preparation so that you are not caught off guard the next time you deal with an offense. Preparation means you try to cover every aspect you can regarding the opponent or subject. The better prepared you are the more likely you will succeed. In preparing to overcome offenses it is vital to know the following:

OFFENSES DEFINED

To overcome an offense you must know what an offense is, and what an offense is not. An offense is much more than a difference of opinion. Everyone has opinions. Opinions about the best brand to buy, the best place to purchase, the best material to use, the best place to go, or the best way to do it. The world is full of different opinions. You will see a difference of opinions in all relationships at some time. No two people see everything identical at all times. A difference of opinion can be healthy. Immaturity makes issues out of opinions. Maturity respects a difference of opinion and moves on. A difference of opinion does not constitute an offense.

When teaching on prayer Jesus dealt with the forgiveness of an offense. In Matthew 6:12 Jesus used the Greek word opheilema which can be translated as debts, sins, or trespasses. These three words can be used interchangeably. You could correctly pray, "Forgive me of my debt as I forgive my debtors," "Forgive me of my sins as I forgive those who sinned against me," or "Forgive me of my trespasses as I forgive those who trespassed against me." All three words carry the meaning of a transgression or violation. An offense is when someone has violated you. This is far greater than a difference of opinion, or doing something differently.

OFFENSES COME

In Luke 17:1 Jesus tells the disciples it is inevitable that offenses will come. To completely understand this statement you have to understand the setting. Jesus was teaching in front of a mixed crowd of tax collectors, sinners, Pharisees, scribes, and disciples. As Jesus began to teach the Pharisees began criticizing him. Pharisees were mean-spirited, religious leaders who were very judgemental. They were Jesus's biggest critics. One of their criticisms of Jesus was for hanging out with sinners and eating with them. The disciples witnessed Jesus dealing with the Pharisee's harshness and disrespect. When Jesus brings up the subject of offenses I believe he was saying, it is impossible in this kind of climate or culture for offenses not to come. Mean, disrespectful, and judgmental Christians cause more offenses in the Kingdom of God than anything else. After having served in pastoral ministry for twenty-four years I can tell you the pharisee spirit is alive today. The pharisee spirit hates spiritual authority and will do anything it can to overthrow it. Churches controlled by people with this spirit will never grow, and will always be in conflict.

Churches that are growing and prospering embrace a culture of acceptance and forgiveness. Churches that are judgmental, harsh, and critical are breeding grounds for offenses. I believe it would be staggering to know how many people in America grew up in church, or were once involved in church, but now no longer attend church because of an offense. It is so sad that the church is often a place where offenses occur. Unfortunately, there are many contributing factors to this from unethical pastors, carnal leadership, or immature Christians. Offenses can cause churches to become dysfunctional, therefore, they never fulfill their purpose of winning people to Christ, making disciples, and equipping believers to do the work of the ministry.

In Luke 17:1 Jesus also gave a warning to those who cause offenses because of the seriousness of it. Jesus used the word "woe" in this verse. Woe is an interjection expressing a denunciation. A denunciation is a warning of impending disaster. It means to take notice, pay attention, and take heed to the warning. There are many woes in scripture. In Matthew 23 alone Jesus pronounces a series of eight woes against the Pharisees and scribes. Offenses produce hurt and division. Proverbs 18:19 teaches us, "A brother offended is harder to win than a strong city." Jesus stated in Matthew 12:25 that every Kingdom, city, or house divided against itself would not stand. One of the primary reasons for division in churches is offenses. The enemy loves to use offenses to continually interrupt the unity of local churches. The Kingdom of God operates through unity. David wrote in Psalm 133:1 "How good and pleasant it is when God's people live together in unity." Unity comes when people rally behind a purpose, not a personality, preference, or perspective. United believers can do amazing things together for the advancement and growth of the Kingdom of God.

OFFENSES ARE TRAPS

The Greek word for offense is skandalon from where we get the words scandal, snare, and trap. An offense is a snare or trap set by the enemy to prevent you from reaching your destiny. In setting traps there are two things an experienced hunter will do. First, the trap will be hidden or covered up so that it is unnoticed. Next, the bait will be placed in the trap to lure an animal into the trap. The animal enters the trap with only the scent of food on its mind not knowing what was about to become of him. This is exactly how Satan works.

In 2 Corinthians 2:5-11, the Apostle Paul wrote about a man who had caused much hurt and also offended the Corinthian Church. He didn't call the man by name but rather identified him as the one who caused much offense. Then Paul said, I have forgiven him, and it is time you forgave him. After that Paul warned the Corinth believers if they didn't forgive the man Satan could take advantage of them because of their unforgiveness. Paul also declared we are not ignorant of Satan's evil schemes. The word ignorant doesn't mean stupid. It means uninformed or unlearned. Ignorance can have negative impacts on people. Hosea 4:6 "My people are destroyed from the lack of knowledge." Paul knew the better you know your enemy, the better you can overcome your enemy. Paul was not speaking of Satan to exalt him, but rather to expose him. Paul was exposing Satan's scheme of trapping the Corinth Church in an offense and robbing them of the destiny of greatness God had for them. Paul was teaching Christians the only way out of the trap of offense is forgiveness.

The trap of offense keeps you weak and struggling. It keeps you from growing, developing, and becoming strong in your faith. After John the Baptist had been arrested, and put in prison Jesus sent him the following message in Matthew 11:6 "Blessed is he who is not offended because of me." Jesus used the word blessed for the one who has been released from the trap of offense by forgiveness. Those who have forgiven an offense are free, and blessed by God.

OFFENSES KEEP YOU UNPRODUCTIVE

In Mark chapter four Jesus identifies Satan as a thief and explains how he steals. In verse 15 Jesus answers five questions.

Question One: Who? The answer is Satan. 1 Peter 5:8 "Be careful! Watch out for attacks from the devil, your great enemy. He prowls around like a roaring lion, looking for some victim to devour."

Question Two: What does he do? He comes. In John 10:10 we read that the thief comes only to "steal, and kill, and destroy."

Question Three: When? "Satan comes immediately," Mark 4:15

Question Four: Why? To steal the word of God. I Peter 1:23 "For you have been born again, not of perishable seed, but of imperishable, through the living and enduring word of God."

Question Five: From where? From their hearts. Romans 10:10 "For with the heart one believes unto righteousness." Faith resides in the heart, not the head. This doesn't mean Christians are to be brain-dead. However, there will be times when the heart and the head are in complete disagreement.

Then Jesus told a story of a farmer who planted seed in four different types of soil, and compared the soil to the human heart. We know that seed produces life and is powerful. All life comes from a seed. Yet, as powerful as the seed is, the soil in which the seed is planted, determines the seed's productivity. Jesus taught about three soil types (hearts) that are unproductive: In verse 16 was the hard heart, in verse 17 was the offended heart, and in verse 19 was the crowded heart. In verse 17 the offended heart had to do with shallow soil. Dirt with no depth. So many offenses come because of immaturity. Mature Christians have depth in their relationship with God and know how to forgive. These three soils (hearts) did not receive the seed (the Word) that was sown, therefore, were not productive. What is so sad is that people with any one of these three hearts are being ripped off by Satan. He uses the hard heart, offended heart, and crowded heart to steal from us the very life-giving seed, or Word, we all so desperately need.

It was only the open heart that received the seed (Word) and brought forth fruit some thirty, some sixty, and some even a hundred times as much as had been planted. The hard heart, offended heart, nor the crowded heart ever produce any fruit. That's how Satan steals, and keeps believers from being productive for the Kingdom of God. Remember, being productive is what brings glory to God (John 15:8), and is a big part of our witness (Matthew 7:20). Your witness is not just what people hear you say, but how people see you live. I encourage you not to live with an offended heart, or Satan will use it against you. Keep an open heart to God so that your life can be productive, and bring glory to God.

OFFENSES CAN LEAD TO A ROOT OF BITTERNESS

Anyone who has worked in lawn care or gardening knows about weeds. There are approximately 250,000 species of plants in the world with an estimated 8,000 of those species considered a weed. The best definition of a weed I have found is, "a plant growing where it is not wanted." One characteristic of a weed is that it reproduces rapidly. The reason for this is that weeds produce an abundance of seeds that are blown about by the wind. That's why weeds seem to show up everywhere. Weeds can do great damage to lawns or gardens because they compete for space, nutrients, water, and light. When dealing with weeds it is important to get to the root of the weed. If you just cut it at ground level you will have a reoccurring problem with the weed, because it is the root of a plant that gives life to a plant.

Offenses, disappointments, brokenness, anger, unforgiveness, and resentment left unresolved lead to bitterness. And that bitterness can go deep into the heart and spirit of a person. Until you deal with the root of bitterness it will continue to reoccur over and over. Hebrews 12:15 "See to it that no one falls short of the grace of God and that no bitter root grows up to cause trouble and defile many."

Roots grow underground most of the time. It is the root system that gives life to a tree or plant. Without roots, there can be no fruit. Fruit grows above the ground making it visible. It's the part of the tree or plant you can't see that produces the fruit you can see. You can see the fruit of bitterness in a person through anger, negative talk, holding grudges, resentment, and a critical spirit. When Peter was dealing with Simon, a man who had been a sorcerer for many years, he said in Acts 8:20-23 "Your heart is not right with God. Turn from your wickedness and pray to The Lord. He will forgive your evil thoughts, for I can see that you are full of bitterness and held captive by sin." Peter could see the fruit of bitterness in Simon. Bitter roots always produce bitter fruit. I am not aware of anything positive bitterness produces.

GOD'S WORD BRINGS HEALING

After one of the greatest miracles recorded in the Bible (God parting the Red Sea), the Israelites traveled three days into the wilderness and found bitter water. While the Israelites were complaining about the bitter water God told Moses to cast a certain tree into the water. Moses did as the Lord instructed him and the waters were changed from bitter to sweet (Exodus 15:22-27). Another great miracle for the Israelites!

Bitterness comes when we continually focus on our hurt and refuse to forgive the offense. The soil of bitterness is a heart that harbors unforgiveness refusing to let it go. The seizure of bitterness is choosing to do away with bitterness at the root so that it doesn't keep reoccurring. As God had a word for Moses and Israel when they were confronted with bitter waters God has a word for everyone today confronting bitterness. It is Ephesians 4:31-32 (NLT) "Get rid of all bitterness, rage, anger, harsh words, and slander, as well as all types of malicious behavior. Instead, be kind to each other, tender-hearted, forgiving one another, just as God through Christ has forgiven you."

When dealing with bitterness you will find healing, strength, and wisdom to overcome offenses in the Word of God. Listen to David in Psalm 119:165 "Great peace has they which love thy law: and nothing shall offend them." God's Word is far more than just a list of dos and don'ts. It is spiritual food for the soul just like natural food is for the body. A healthy diet of natural food supplies our bodies with the energy and strength it needs daily. A balanced diet of the word of God is strength and healing for our spirit man. That is why when Jesus was being tempted (Matthew 4:4) he quoted Deuteronomy 8:3 "People need more than bread for their life; they must feed on every word of God."

In Psalm 19:10 and Psalm 119:103, David compares the word of God to honey. Honey is a sweet syrup-like substance that bees produce from the nectar of flowering plants. The bees collect the nectar, consume it, digest it, and regurgitate it inside the beehive to produce honey. Honey is the only food produced by an insect

.   Honey has numerous health benefits associated with it. Honey is rich in antioxidants that help fight cancer, improves cholesterol which is good for your heart, lowers blood pressure, helps with digestive issues, reduces allergy symptoms, heals sore throats, and can even help you sleep. Honey is very nutritious in so many ways, and very good for you.

One other benefit of honey is that it is a natural sweetener. If added or put into other foods or drinks that have a bitter taste honey can take away in a great measure the bitterness. Life often has the bitter taste of offenses in it. The Word of God is a natural sweetener that can reduce the bitterness of offenses. Here are three scriptures that were very sweet to me when dealing with bitterness: Psalm 147:3 "He heals the brokenhearted and binds up their wounds;" Isaiah 54:17 "No weapon forged against you will prevail;" Romans 8:28 "We know that in all things God works for the good of those who love him, who have been called according to his purpose."

With Psalm 147:3 I knew God would not leave me broken. With Isaiah 54:17, I knew God would not let what happened to destroy me. With Romans 8:28 I knew God didn't cause it, but would work it for my good.

Those three scriptures helped me in a very bitter time of my life and reassured me that God was not done with me, and I still had a future. Now that is sweet! As the old Hymn says, "Tis so sweet to trust in Jesus."

IT'S YOUR CHOICE

You can't control everything that comes to you in life, but you can control how you respond to it. One of the best ways to deal with an offense is to let it go. Determine within yourself not to allow offenses to control you. If you don't, offenses will control you. Anger and frustration will dominate your world. Proverbs 19:11 "A person's wisdom yields patience; it is to one's glory to overlook an offense." Notice from this scripture that choosing not to live in an offense is about self-control. It's about me, not what was done to me. Patience and self-control are listed as part of the Fruit of the Spirit in Galatians 5:22-23. The Holy Spirit gives the patience, and self-control to deal with offenses.

Anger is an emotion we all have. We see in the Bible that God became angry with Israel on several occasions. Jesus became angry when money changers turned the Temple into a flea market. The Bible doesn't say anger is a sin. It says anger out of control is a sin. Anger channeled in the right direction can produce good things. Listen to Ephesians 4:26-27, "Don't sin by letting anger gain control over you. Don't let the sun go down while you are still angry, for anger gives a mighty foothold to the devil." Anger out of control overreacts, jumps to conclusions, assumes the worst, says things it shouldn't, refuses to reason, and does much damage.

James 1:19-20 tells us everyone should be quick to listen, slow to speak, and slow to become angry. This is self-control. This is our goal. The Holy Spirit will help us so that we control our anger and respond in a constructive way, not a destructive way. When possible overlooking an offense is the best way of dealing with it. There are times when you do need to respond to an offense, and the Holy Spirit will help you do it in a Biblical way that is orderly, peaceful, and graceful.

The greatest example of self-control is when Jesus was being nailed to the cross by Roman soldiers he prayed a prayer of forgiveness for them. He had spoken earlier about control in John 10:18. "No one can take my life from me. I sacrifice it voluntarily. For I have the authority to lay it down when I want to and also to take it up again." The soldiers didn't take his life, he laid down his life. The pressure of the moment did not cause Jesus to lose control. His choice to lie down on the cross revealed his control. When the heat is on and the pressure mounts remember you choose how to respond. My response reveals if an offense is controlling me or if the Fruit of the Spirit (self-control) is at work in me. It's all about my choice.

CHAPTER 9

MASTERING MISTAKES

We all make mistakes. No one is exempt. The best athletes make them. The smartest in the profession make them. The most experienced in the field make them. Mistakes can be made with the best of intentions. Mistakes can be made even after prayer, planning, and preparation. Sometimes mistakes come from being careless, not paying attention, not concentrating, or poor judgment. Mistakes in marriage, parenting, relationships, finances, on the job, and the list goes on and on. You will even make mistakes going through recovery. I certainly made mine. Some mistakes are worse than others and carry greater consequences. Mistakes teach us that we are all human, and no one reaches perfection in this life.

David was thirty years old when he became King of the tribe of Judah. He served Judah for seven and a half years. Then he became King of all of Israel and served in that leadership role for thirty-three years. When he became King of all of Israel one of his first desires was to bring back the Ark of the Covenant from the Philistines. The Philistines had captured the Ark while in battle with the Israelites and kept it in several locations before taking it to Abinadab's house where it had remained for twenty years. The dimensions of the Ark of the Covenant were: 3&3/4 feet long, 2&1/4 feet wide, and 2&1/4 feet high (Exodus 25:10-16). It contained two tablets (Commandments of God), a rod (Authority of God), and a jar of manna (Provision of God). It was built of wood, overlaid with gold inside and out. It probably weighed about 200 to 300 pounds. God's designated place for the Ark of the Covenant was in the Tabernacle's Holy of Holies. It represented God's tangible presence. Israel had carried it with them during their forty-year journey in the wilderness.

David's intentions were good, but he made a costly mistake. David consulted with Israel's political leaders instead of the Lord (1 Chronicles 13:1-14). Instead of asking the Levites/Priests to carry the Ark of the Covenant on their shoulders as was how the Ark was to be transported (1 Chronicles 15:11-15) David followed the example of the Philistines, and put the Ark of the

Covenant on a new cart pulled by oxen. As David and his men were returning the Ark to Jerusalem and celebrating along the way one of the oxen stumbled. When the ox stumbled, Uzzah, the driver of the cart, put his hand on the Ark of the Covenant to steady it. No man was allowed to touch the Ark because it represented the glory of God. When Uzzah placed his hand on the Ark God struck him dead. Now a man is dead because David made the mistake of not following God's way of transporting the Ark of the Covenant to Jerusalem. David has to take some time and regroup from this horrible mistake. The next time David attempted to transport the Ark of the Covenant back to Jerusalem he did it God's way, and it was successful (2 Samuel 5-6, 1 Chronicles 13-15).

What did David learn from his costly mistake? First, he learned to pay attention to doing life in God's way. David's desire to return the Ark of the Covenant to Jerusalem was admirable. In the excitement of bringing back the Ark David was neglectful of God's way to transport it, and did it his way. When we are determined to do life our way is when we usually make our greatest mistakes. Make sure the decisions you make in life line up with God's way. We know God's way by His Word (Bible). Study it, and learn God's way to live life. God's Word has the answer for every issue in life. God's way is always the best. God's way brings fulfillment, contentment, joy, peace, and success.

Secondly, David learned he could try again. After taking some time and reevaluating his mistake David decided to try again. His passion for returning the Ark was greater than the failure of his first attempt. When your passion is greater than your failure you will succeed. Most successful people have failed many times. I admired David for trying again after his painful mistake. His second attempt at returning the Ark was successful because he learned from the mistake of his first attempt at returning the Ark. Mistakes can teach you some great lessons. Learn from your mistakes, and try again.

Mistakes can destroy you, or develop you. It depends on how you handle them. The word mastering means to acquire a skill or gain control of it. If you master something you have learned how to do it. You have become proficient in the use of something. An example would be a person who mastered the art of cooking. This person has cooked long enough to know what ingredients to use, which spices to put in, how to mix the ingredients, what temperature, how long to cook a dish, and the art of putting a meal together.

In recovering from your past you can make mistakes. Your intentions can be good and still make mistakes. Don't let a mistake keep you from your recovery. Learn from it, and try again. So much of recovery is trying again. Winston Churchill was a great leader, and said, "Success is not final; failure is not fatal: It is the courage to continue that counts." God can help you master your mistakes. Romans 8:28 states, "God works all things for our good." "All things" includes our mistakes. If your struggling with some mistakes you've made here are seven steps that will assist you in mastering them.

ADMIT IT

Only pride would keep a person from admitting they were wrong and made a mistake. Pride can keep a person from being true to themselves which will hurt their ability to work through difficulties. Pride sets you up for failure. Remember, pride goes before a fall.

OWN IT

Accept full responsibility for your mistake. Don't try to pass the buck, or play the blame game. Blaming someone else, or something else for your mistake is the easy way out, and never deals with the real issues you may be having. Cowards blame while people of courage own it!

CORRECT IT

Do everything you can to correct your mistake, and make it right if at all possible. Go the second mile to make things right. It is never too late to do the right thing. One day you will look back and be so glad you did.

APOLOGIZE FOR IT

If your mistake hurt someone go directly to them, and give them a real, heartfelt I'm sorry. Don't wait, and don't put it off. The sooner you apologize the better it will be for the person you hurt, and you. Apologies can go a long way in restoring the damage done by mistakes in relationships.

LEARN FROM IT

Let this become a learning experience. The pain of mistakes can be a great teacher. If you don't learn from it, you most likely will repeat it. If you continually make the same mistake, it is not a mistake any longer. It is a choice.

GROW FROM IT

This is an opportunity for you to grow and mature as a person. Don't waste it. Growing up is God's way of preparing us for our future, and will play an important role in you fulfilling your purpose in life.

MOVE ON FROM IT

You can't live with your mistake forever. You may always remember your mistake, but you don't have to live with it forever. After you have done all of the above (numbers 1-6) move on. Moving on means leaving the regrets of past mistakes, and focusing on your future and its rewards much wiser and stronger.

CHAPTER 10

BREAKING INFLUENCES

Memories, flashbacks, dates, names, holidays, pictures, songs, and events can trigger painful emotions from traumatic experiences from your past. It can happen quickly and unexpectedly. The influence of what happened can be with you for years. In 2012 while I was ministering in Georgia I had lunch with two pastor friends one day. As we were eating one of the pastors shared his story of how he had lost a marriage due to his wife's unfaithfulness and abandonment seventeen years earlier. He had married again and was doing well in marriage and ministry. Yet, as he shared his story tears began to flow down his face, and I could sense the hurt in his voice. For whatever reason on that day the influence of a horrible experience brought back such pain he couldn't hide it. Just when you think you have conquered it, it's back again! Old wounds can resurface, and cause you much grief. Getting past the past is not easy because your enemy, Satan, loves to use it against you. In Revelation 12:11 Satan is named the "Accuser" who is making accusations at the people of God 24/7. The "Accuser" loves to drag up your past to keep you discouraged and defeated even when you have moved on in life.

Living under the influence of your past is as dangerous emotionally as driving an automobile under the influence of alcohol is physically. Drunk driving is extremely dangerous because it impairs vision, alters decision-making, and slows reflexes. It is the same for a person living under the influence of their past emotionally. They often can't see a situation clearly which means their perception of reality is off. Decision-making becomes inconsistent and questionable. Responding to normal challenges can seem overwhelming.

Some examples of people who are tormented by negative influences from their past could be Veterans who can't sleep because of terrible nightmares of a war that took place years ago. Women who had an abortion and grieve the child who would be a teenager now. A business owner who lost everything because of poor choices and is now living with regrets. An athlete who had a promising career, but lost it all because of a drug addiction, and now can only dream of what could have been. The person who can't keep a job because of alcoholism, and is never able to reach their full potential and it haunts them. The dad who never had the relationship with his children he should have and deals with the remorse of not being there for them even after they're grown. Influences from the past can be powerfully negative, and drain the life out of a person.

While breaking the influences of the past can be a battle at times, it can be done. In Philippians 3:12-14 the Apostle Paul gives us a great success formula for living life. He makes it very clear that he is nowhere close to perfection, but he is forgetting those things which are behind, reaching forward to those things which were ahead, and pressing toward the goal for the prize of the call of God in Christ Jesus. Paul's success formula consists of three words: forgetting, reaching, and pressing. Forgetting had to do with the past. Reaching is dealing with the present. Pressing is focusing on the future. With all the great books on how to be successful on the market today, I believe Paul's formula for success is the best one you will find.

The word forgetting in Philippians 3:13 means, to not recall information concerning some particular matter. Pastor and author Warren Wiersbe did a comprehensive study of Philippians in his book, Be Joyful. He states that the Greek word for forgetting goes much deeper than failing to recall. It means, "no longer controlled by," or "no longer influenced by." So it is greater than forgetting where you put your keys or phone, forgetting someone's birthday, or not recalling where you parked your car at the mall. It is getting to the place you can say my past no longer controls me or influences me. It is a great day when you can make that statement.

The statement "no longer controlled by" or "no longer influenced by" is coming from a man who had a terrible past. Paul writes about his past in 1 Timothy 1:13-15. In verse 13 he confessed that he formerly was a blasphemer, persecutor, and a violent aggressor. He hated Christianity with a passion. He was the church's number one enemy and did everything he could to harm Christians. In verse 15 Paul describes himself as the "chief of sinners," or the "worst of sinners." He used the word "worst" to describe himself and his past.

In Acts chapter nine, a man named Saul was on his way to Damascus to arrest Christians and take them to prison in Jerusalem. On his way, Jesus appeared to him with a bright light, and He asked Saul, "Why are you persecuting me?" Saul was converted to Christ, and the Lord changes his name from Saul to Paul. Saul is a Hebrew name that means, "ask or question." Paul is Latin which means, "humble or small." The conversion took him from Saul who was always asking and questioning, to Paul who was humble and small. This was preparation for a man God was about to use mighty for his Kingdom.

After his conversion, Paul was blind for three days due to the bright light shone when Jesus appeared to him. Some of Paul's friends lead him to Damascus where he stayed for the next three days. While Paul was in Damascus The Lord spoke to a man named Ananias to go find Paul and lay his hands on him and pray for him. Ananias had heard of Paul and his reputation for violence, and was reluctant to go find Paul. However, The Lord reassured Ananias saying, "Go for he is a chosen vessel unto me." (verse 15) The man who had a past so bad he described himself as the "worst of sinners" is now "a chosen vessel unto The Lord." At his conversion, Paul discovered his purpose in life. Your purpose in life will always be found in Christ. Paul's purpose answered the two questions he asked laying on the Damascus road. In verse 5 Paul asked Jesus, "Who are you?" In verse 6 Paul asked Jesus, "What do you want me to do?" Your purpose will identify that Jesus is the Son of God, and what you are to do for the Kingdom of God. Saul was a religious fanatic and the worst of sinners who became Paul at his conversion.

Paul became the Apostle to the Gentiles, a great missionary, and authored the majority of the New Testament.

Years later in writing his second letter to believers in Corinth Paul makes a powerful statement concerning conversion in II Corinthians 5:17 "If anyone is in Christ, he is a new creation; old things have passed away; behold, all things have become new."

Old things passing away are the sins of the old life. In Christ, you have a new beginning, but it doesn't end there. God is continually making you new. Even if you have been a Christian for years God is still at work in you (Philippians 1:6) perfecting you into newness.

A new creation is not God just cleaning up our old nature, and making it look the best it can. It is God creating a new you. I have told the story of a friend of mine who owned a car repair shop named Jeff. Jeff kept my car serviced and running for many years. When a part of my car like an alternator was worn out and needed to be replaced he would send me to a junkyard to buy the part to help with the repair cost. One day as we were talking I asked Jeff, do you realize half my car came out of the junkyard? We had a good laugh about it. When you were born again God made you a new creation. You are not a collection of old used parts from the junkyard of the past. Old things are past. All things are new. That's why a Christian with a terrible past can get to the place he can say, my past doesn't control me or influence me.

Forgetting doesn't mean the past didn't happen. It doesn't mean the event didn't take place. It doesn't mean the offenses didn't occur. It doesn't mean the hurt wasn't real. Forgetting means you have grown through it all, and have come to the place you can now say, the past no longer controls me. Bad memories no longer influence you, your decisions, or your future. Getting to the point of not being controlled by the past is so freeing.

Forgetting doesn't mean there are no painful moments. The story of Joseph is found in Genesis 37-50. It is an amazing account of how his brothers were jealous of him, robbed him of his beautiful coat of many colors, threw him in a pit, and sold him for slavery. Thirteen years later, God promoted Joseph to be Governor of Egypt. His brothers came to Egypt to inquire about food because of a great famine in the land. Joseph received word his brothers were there and set up a meeting with them. Once he was alone with his brothers, he broke down and wept. He cried hysterically and sobbed so loudly he could be heard throughout Pharaoh's palace (Genesis 45). After all that his brothers had done to him, Joseph's pain was so great that his emotions overtook him and he had a temporary meltdown. After regaining his composure he identified himself to his brothers. His brothers were in such shock that Joseph had to identify himself twice, saying, "I am Joseph, your brother, whom you sold into slavery." While Joseph felt the pain of the past, he didn't allow the pain of the past to control him or influence him. He didn't use the past against his brothers as an excuse to send them home empty-handed. He loved his brothers and blessed them with more than enough supplies to survive the famine. Then Joseph instructed his brothers to go home and return with their elderly father. His brothers brought their father, Jacob, to Egypt, and we see a beautiful picture of reconciliation between Joseph, his father, and his brothers (Genesis 46). This story could have ended much differently if Joseph had allowed the pain of his past to control or influence his decision-making. In breaking the negative influences of the past off of your life you need to consider several important things.

PROTECT YOUR MIND

There will always be memories and flashbacks. The goal is to dismiss any negative thoughts that would bring you to anger, and regretful behavior. Protect your thought life by using Philippians 4:8 as your guide: "Fix your thoughts on what is true and honorable and right. Think about things that are pure and lovely and admirable. Think about things that are excellent and worthy of praise."

Protecting your mind needs to be a priority because that is where strongholds develop. In Greek, the stronghold is a military word synonymous with fortress or prison. It refers to an area where the enemy has become entrenched. Ephesians 6:17 instructs us to put on the helmet of salvation. Helmets are for protection. Romans 12:2 teaches us not to be conformed to the world, but to be transformed by the renewing of our minds. Sometimes we have to be deprogrammed and reprogrammed to think right. Why is this so important? The answer is in Proverbs 23:7 which tells us as a man thinks so is he.

The emphasis from 2 Corinthians 10:3-5 is that one of the keys to victorious living is taking control of your thinking. The way we do that is by using God's mighty weapons to pull down strongholds in our minds. These weapons will break down every proud argument that keeps us from knowing God, and conquer rebellious ideals teaching them to obey Christ.

Taking control of your thought life is possible. I had a man who once told me he couldn't control how or what he thought. I responded with this illustration: if I'm watching television and something comes on I don't want to see I have to decide whether to leave the channel where it is and watch it anyway, change the channel, or turn the television off. With my remote, I control what I watch. When unwholesome thoughts come into your mind you can entertain them or dismiss them. The choice is yours. One of the fruits of the Spirit is self-control. The Holy Spirit helps us control the way we think, talk, behave, and respond. Solomon told us in Proverbs 25:28 (NLT) "A person without self-control is as defenseless as a city with broken-down walls." The self-control of your thinking is a major key to breaking negative influences from your life.

SPEAK LIFE

Proverbs 18:21 (NIV) "The tongue has the power of life and death." We all can speak life over ourselves or death over ourselves. In James chapter 3, we find that the tongue is more powerful than most people think.

1. It Can Chart Our Course (verses 1-4). James compares the tongue to two small devices that when used can give control and direction. A small bit enables a rider to control and directs a large horse. A small rudder enables a pilot to control and direct a large ship. While the tongue is a small member of the human body it has the power to control and direct our course in life.

2. Destroy What Is Valuable (verses 5-8). James compares the tongue to a fire and a dangerous animal which both can be very destructive. A fire can begin with a small spark and destroy a forest, a home, a building, or a community. It spreads and destroys. The destruction of a home due to fire often includes valuables such as pictures, documents, or personal belongings that can never be replaced. The tongue is also like a dangerous animal that is relentless in seeking its prey and destroying it. It is very unfortunate to hear reports of campers, or hikers being attacked by a bear or a mountain lion. Words like fire or wild animals can be very destructive. How many valuable friendships and relationships have been destroyed because of the tongue?

3. Provide Health For The Soul (verses 9-12). James compares the tongue to a fountain providing clean, cool, water, and a tree producing beautiful fruit. In Bible days a well was a great blessing to a village. Water is a necessity for life. Without water, dehydration sets in and leads to serious health issues. Our words can be like a fountain giving life. The tongue is also like a tree. Trees are very important for many reasons. One of the main reasons is that they bear fruit. Fruit is one of the healthiest foods you can eat. The fountain and the tree are life-giving and refreshing. That's how our words can be to our souls: life-giving

and refreshing! Proverbs 18:4 (NLT) "A person's words can be life-giving water; words of true wisdom are as refreshing as a bubbling brook."

Our words can chart our course, destroy what is valuable, or provide health to our souls. The choice is ours. I hope you will speak life-giving words that will chart your course, protect what is valuable to you, and provide health for your soul.

FOCUS ON YOUR FUTURE

At the age of 120, Moses died (Deuteronomy 34). This was a major blow for Israel. Their great leader Moses is dead. It was Moses whom God called to leadership from a burning bush. It was Moses who confronted Pharaoh to release Israel after 430 years of slavery. It was Moses who led Israel out of Egypt. It was Moses who stood at the Red Sea stretching out his rod and God dividing the water for Israel to walk across on dry sand. It was Moses who led Israel into the wilderness. It was Moses who climbed to the top of Mount Sinai, and received the Ten Commandments from God. There had never been another prophet like Moses. What a leader, and what a loss for Israel. Israel mourns and weeps for Moses for the next 30 days. For a month the people of Israel did nothing but grieve for Moses. Deuteronomy 34:8-9 tells us that when the customary period of mourning was over God called Joshua to step into the leadership role Moses had filled. In Joshua 1:2 God speaks to Joshua to lead Israel across the Jordan River and go to the Promise Land. Now God has changed their focus from the past to the future. Where you are going is more important than where you've been. Where you are going is more important than what you've lost. Your destiny is ahead not behind you. Don't allow influences from the past to keep you tied to the past. No matter how great or bad someone's past is, they can't live in it. Transitioning means leaving the influences of yesterday and moving forward into your tomorrow. The transition of Moses to Joshua teaches us to focus on the future by reminding us that change is inevitable.

Life doesn't stay the same for anyone. Your journey in life will be filled with seasons, changes, and transitions. Everything in life is temporary except Christ, his Word, and His Kingdom. Transitions brought about by loss are extremely difficult and painful. Accepting the reality that life isn't going to be the same can be overwhelming, to say the least. Life without Moses was going to be different. Joshua turned out to be a great leader, but he wasn't Moses. Change comes with life. Some changes are positive and healthy. Some changes are negative and difficult. Regardless of the cause, change happens.

1. Mourning is needed when going through change. Mourning loss is natural. It takes time to say goodbye. Grieving is a process. Processing is working it out, working through it, and coming to terms with it over, and over, and over again. After experiencing loss it is dangerous not to grieve. Living in denial never leads to recovery. Emotions that have not been dealt with can cause great distress. The grief process involves feeling the pain, the anger, and the disappointment to heal emotionally. God knew before Israel could move forward with Joshua they had to mourn Moses.

2. Moving on is a necessity. God gave Israel 30 days to mourn Moses and then called Joshua to lead because their journey wasn't finished. The thirty days were a time out for them. Grieving is not limited to several days or a certain period, but allows one's heart to express the sorrow that comes from loss. One of the challenges of grieving is not getting stuck in it. You can get stuck in the past and pain. God would not allow Israel to stay in mourning in the plains of Moab because it would forfeit them from reaching their destination of the Promise Land. Yes, grieving can last for more than thirty days, but there will come a day it is time to move on. If you don't you will be the loser. Israel's moving on was in no way disrespectful to Moses, but a

continuation of their journey to the Promise Land. Moving on takes faith because you do not know everything that is ahead of you. Moving on doesn't mean you have all the answers. A great compass for navigating your future when you are not sure of tomorrow is Proverbs 3:5-6 "Trust in The Lord with all your heart; do not depend on your own understanding. Seek His will in all you do, and He will direct your paths."

CHAPTER 11

PEACE WITH YOUR PAST

The movie, Forest Gump, opened in theaters on July 6, 1994, becoming an instant success, and the biggest box-office hit of the year. The character of Forest Gump has become a cultural icon. The movie has many great scenes, and famous lines such as when Forest is sitting on a park bench with a woman and says to her, "Life is like a box of chocolates, you never know what you're going to get."

One of the greatest scenes is when Forest and Jenny are out taking a walk together. Jenny was Forest's childhood friend and the woman he loved. As they are walking they come to the house where Jenny grew up. Looking at the old house Jenny becomes very angry and upset. She runs towards the house and begins picking up rocks and throwing them at the house. Seeing the house brings back a flood of horrific memories for Jenny. It was in that house that a young, innocent Jenny was abused and violated by her father. From that abuse, she turned to a lifestyle of alcoholism and drugs going from relationship to relationship with men. After her outburst of anger, Jenny falls to the ground crying. She is emotionally distraught from memories of abuse that still haunted her. Trying to console her Forest sits down beside Jenny on the dirt road, and said to her, "Sometimes I guess there just aren't enough rocks."

Jenny throwing rocks at the old house was an outward behavior triggered by inward-damaged emotions and unresolved anger. It was all she knew to do at the moment. However, throwing rocks at her past, no matter how painful it was, didn't change it, or bring emotional healing to her. Forest was right when he said, sometimes there just aren't enough rocks! As much as Jenny hated what happened in that house throwing rocks at it was not the answer. Throwing rocks was evidence that what had happened years earlier still tormented her, and that time by itself hadn't brought healing and wholeness. Jenny's past of abuse and unresolved anger was destroying her, and she didn't know how to deal with it.

How do you find peace with your past when it is ugly? How do you overcome a part of your life that you hate? How do you rise above what brought you so much pain? How do you bring resolve to a hurt that caused so much damage? How do you believe good can come from a grievous offense? These types of questions can be answered by Isaiah 61:3.

The Prophet Isaiah had a message for the Jewish people who were suffering in his day. Isaiah 61:3 "He will give a crown of beauty for ashes." Ashes were symbolic of deep grief. It was customary in Isaiah's day for people who had loss, pain, or distress to sit and cover themselves in ashes as a sign of mourning. Isaiah's message to hurting people was God will replace their ashes for beauty. The beauty for ashes message means that:

- God will not leave you like you are.
- God can bring healing and wholeness to you.
- Ashes represent defeat. A crown represents victory. God can replace your defeat with victory.
- Defeat is temporary. Don't get accustomed to living in ashes. God has a beautiful crown waiting for you.

Isaiah talked about God doing his part for you to have peace with your past. Now you have to do your part. You have to cooperate with God. Philippians 2:12-13 seems to be a paradox at first, but it's not. Verse 12 tells us to "work out your salvation with fear and trembling." Then verse 13 reads, "It is God who works in you to will and to act to fulfill his good pleasure." Two agents are working together for God's will and the best to be accomplished for you: God and you. There must be a cooperative effort on your part for you to come to peace with your past.

In cooperating with God to make peace with your past you need to do the following:

LEAN ON GOD'S GRACE

The Apostle Paul discovered God's grace and wrote about it in 2 Corinthians 12: 7-10. Paul was dealing with a situation he couldn't change. He even prayed three times, and nothing changed. It was such a painful time he referred to it as a thorn in his flesh. God didn't answer Paul's prayer as Paul wanted. God's answer to Paul's prayer is in verse 9 (NLT) "My grace is all you need. My power works best in weakness." While Paul is hurting and unable to make changes he discovers God's grace. God didn't remove his pain but gave Paul grace. God's grace is the power for living that gives you the ability to deal with your hurts, failures, and disappointments in life. Paul's solution to a painful situation he couldn't change was grace. Grace gives you the courage to try again, the strength to face what you can't change, and the endurance to stand under pressure. God's grace is always greater!

John Newton was born July 24, 1725, in London, England. His mother died two weeks before his seventh birthday. His father was a commander of a merchant ship that sailed the Mediterranean Sea. Newton took his first sea voyage with his father at age eleven. During his teenage years, he pursued life at sea and became known for his rebellion, cruelty, and foul mouth. In 1747 Newton was aboard the Greyhound sailing the North Atlantic when the ship was overtaken by a violent storm that last more than a week. During the storm, Newton cried out to God for mercy and later claimed this was the turning point of his life.

Newton then served as a mate, and as a captain of many slave ships hoping as a Christian to restrain the worst excesses of the slave trade. He left the ship for an office job in 1755 and began to hold Bible studies in his home in Liverpool. During this time of conducting Bible studies, Newton began writing hymns. He wrote a total of 281 hymns with Amazing Grace being the most famous. In 1757 he applied for the Anglican Priesthood and was denied. Believing God had called him into ministry Newton persisted with the priesthood, and was finally accepted in 1764.

John Newton became increasingly disgusted with the Slave Trade, and his role in it. In 1787 he wrote, "Thoughts upon the African Slave Trade" which graphically described the horrors of the Slave Trade. Later he joined the campaign to abolish the Slave Trade. In February 1807 when the act to abolish the Slave Trade finally became law Newton who was nearly blind, and near death "rejoiced to hear the wonderful news." The man who was a part of the Slave Trade ended up despising it, worked to end it, and witnessed its destruction before his death the very same year, December 1807.

Grace will change you. It changed John Newton. He had experienced God's grace in such a manner he had to write about it. He wrote a song that has been sung by Christians all over the world for over 200 years. I believe the reason for its enormous popularity is that Christians relate and identify with Amazing Grace.

The song has four great verses. When I read the lyrics I'm reading the words of a man who found saving grace in verse 1. "Amazing Grace, how sweet the sound, that saved a wretch like me. I once was lost, but now am found, was blind but now I see." And found living grace in verse 3. "Through many dangers, toils, and snares I have already come. Tis Grace has brought me safe thus far, and Grace will lead us home." If you are going to make peace with your past you have to discover God's grace.

LEARN TO PRAY

In Luke 11, just after Jesus had finished a time of prayer one of his disciples approached him saying teach us to pray. It was a great request. Prayer is essential to coming to peace with your past. In learning to pray there are three dynamics of prayer you need to know.

1. The person – Prayer revolves around the person of Jesus. Prayer is not based upon rituals, ceremonies, or traditions but on the person of Jesus Christ. In the book of Hebrews chapters four and five Jesus is identified as our Priest. A Priest is a person called by God to bring people to God. He represents them to God in all their sins, needs, and sacrifices. We have a Priest who understands our struggles, temptations, and weaknesses. The reason Jesus understands is because He left heaven and came to earth. On earth, Jesus encountered Satan, temptation, rejection, betrayal, accusations, criticism, opposition, and suffering. If Jesus had not come to earth He would have never experienced any of this because none of the before mentioned is in heaven. So Jesus understands us because he became one of us without taking on our sinful nature. Jesus never sinned because He didn't have an earthly father. Jesus did not carry the DNA of a man. Jesus carried His Heavenly Father's DNA and had no sin. While he was sinless he still experienced the hurts and pains of life. That's why He understands our hurts and pains.

Where is our Priest? In Hebrews 8:1 we read that Jesus is seated at the right hand of the Father at the Throne of Majesty in heaven which means Jesus is at the place of highest honor in heaven. After His crucifixion, Jesus was buried in a tomb for 3 days. He arose from the dead on the third day and spent the next 40 days teaching and mentoring the disciples about the Kingdom of God. He ascended back to heaven and sat down at the right hand of the Father on His throne because His earthly mission was completed. A throne represents authority and majesty. Our Priest is not on a cross, or in a tomb, he is on the throne! When we pray to our Priest we should always allow our mind and spirit to take us to His throne.

2. The place – Jesus also taught about our place of prayer in Matthew 6:6 as a closet. In prayer, Jesus' place is at the right hand of the throne, and our place is in a closet. The word closet can also be interpreted as a bedchamber. Both places represent privacy or intimacy. We need alone time with The Lord without

the distractions of life which is why Jesus instructed us to shut the door. We need a place of privacy and intimacy with the Lord. On August 28, 2015, the Christian drama film, War Room, was released in American theaters, and received generally negative reviews from critics, but became a box office success. A young mother (Elizabeth) on the verge of losing her marriage is taught about the War Room (a closet) by a great senior woman of faith (Miss Clara). By developing her own War Room (a closet) Elizabeth saved her marriage. Eventually, Elizabeth, her daughter, Danielle, and her husband, Tony, learned together the blessing of having a closet.

3. The power - When Jesus taught his disciples to pray he taught them a powerful prayer. It is recorded in Matthew 6:9-13 and Luke 11:2-4. It is the only prayer Jesus taught his disciples to pray. It is a powerful prayer that consists of:

Relationship: "Our Father in Heaven." We have the privilege of addressing God as our Father which means we are his children. Children come into a family by birth or adoption. Both concepts are in scripture. Birth is found in John 3:3-7, 1 John 2:29, 3:9, 4:7, 5:1,4,18. Adoption is in Romans 8:15-16, Galatians 4:4-7, and Ephesians 1:5. Both concepts have to do with entrance. A child can enter a family by birth or adoption. Either entrance brings the same privileges and rights. A birth child or adopted child both have the privilege of saying, Father. Both concepts are the work of the Holy Spirit. Whichever one speaks to you entitles you to address God as your Father.

Honor - "Hallowed be your name." To honor means to hold in high esteem or great respect. The third commandment had to do with holding God's name in high esteem by not taking it in vain or misusing it. Exodus 20:7

Invitation - "Your kingdom come and your will be done." The invitation is how you bring heaven to earth. When you receive an invitation it means your presence is desired. By praying prayers of invitation we are letting God know His presence is desired in our lives, marriages, and families.

Provision – "Give us this day our daily bread." We petition our Father for provision with full assurance according to Matthew 7:11 "If you then, being evil, know how to give good gifts to your children, how much more will your Father who is in heaven give good things to those who ask him!"

Forgiveness – "Forgive us our debts as we forgive our debtors." Asking for forgiveness of our debts while giving forgiveness to our debtors will maintain a continual flow of the love and grace of Christ in our lives. Forgiveness is not a one-time event, it is a continual experience. Ephesians 4:32 "Be kind to each other, tenderhearted, forgiving one another, just as God through Christ has forgiven you."

Protection – "Lead us not into temptation but deliver us from the evil one."

Jesus called us sheep in John 10:14. Sheep are animals with no natural defenses.

Dogs and cats have claws. Eagles and hawks have talons. Bears and lions have powerful jaws and teeth. Snakes have poisonous fangs. The only defense sheep have is their shepherd. Our only defense against the evil one is Jesus! Pray for protection over your marriage, children, family, health, finances, church, pastor, country, and leaders.

Praise – "For thine is the kingdom, and the power, and the glory, forever." Amen. Luke didn't record this statement of praise, but it is found in Matthew 6:13. The reason I listed it is that I don't think prayer is complete without praise.

Your praise completes your prayer. As powerful as this prayer is, it gets even greater with praise. Praise always adds. Praise is the exclamation point! Concluding prayer with praise will bring results.

LET IT GO

One of the most popular disciples was Simon Peter. Peter and his brother, Andrew were commercial fishermen. One day Peter and Andrew were fishing at the Sea of Galilee. As they were casting a net Jesus was walking along the shore and said to them, follow me and I will make you fishers of men. Their response was immediately to lay down their nets and go with Jesus. Take note that Peter and Andrew never hesitated to lay down their livelihood to follow Christ. They had no idea what was happening, or what they were about to be a part of, but they were willing to follow. This was the beginning of Jesus' earthly ministry. Jesus had been confirmed at His baptism in the river Jordan by the Father. Jesus had been led into the wilderness by the Holy Spirit where He fasted forty days, and overcame the temptation of the devil by quoting the Word of God. Jesus had begun preaching the message of salvation, and the Kingdom of God. Now He is walking along the shores of the Sea of Galilee and selects His first two disciples. Jesus chooses two everyday common, dirty, maybe stinking men, to be on His Board of Directors. These guys didn't have expensive suits and ties. They didn't come out of some plush office complex. Neither did they have a formal education. These men were only familiar with nets and boats since fishing was their trade, and yet Jesus chose them and called them to be His first disciples. It is amazing what God can do with everyday common people who are willing to follow!

For the next three and a half years Peter and Andrew were a part of the ministry of Jesus. They were involved in and witnessed the miracles and healings Jesus performed. They were there at the crucifixion. They saw Him after His resurrection. They witnessed His ascension. They were in the upper room when the Holy Spirit was poured out on the 120 believers. They were apostles in the early church for years after Jesus had returned to heaven. Two common fishermen are now statesmen of the faith because they left their nets and became fishers of men. They died in the faith. Andrew was crucified, and Peter was crucified upside down. Little did these two brothers know that day Jesus called out to them at the Sea of Galilee they were following a King, and would be a part of His Kingdom that would never end.

Before his death, Peter wrote a letter of encouragement to believers who were suffering great hardships and persecution because of their faith. First Peter is an amazing book about trials, tests, and determination. There is one simple little verse in chapter five that can improve your life immensely. I Peter 5:7 states, "Casting all your cares upon Him, for He cares for you. In this verse we see the fisherman's mentality coming out of Peter after all those years. The word casting means releasing. A good fisherman knew that much of his success would be in how he cast his net. A bad or poor cast would probably mean there would not be much to take to market that day which would affect their pay. No casting was a sure failure. Every fisherman knows you can't hold the net in your hands and expect to catch fish. You can starve to death with a net in your hands. There has to be a release to have success!

In counseling, there is a part of recovery called release. There are people much more qualified than me that will tell you before you can get over an offense or hurt you must release it. You can't hold on to an offense, and overcome the offense at the same time. The power of release is that you have an opportunity to let go of an offense and have an opportunity for success at the same time.

The ancient Roman Emperors were notorious for hideous forms of punishment for criminals. One horrible form was the binding of a murder victim to the back of the murderer. By law, no one was allowed to remove the corpse from the condemned person. As the dead body begins to decay and decompose its toxins and poisons would enter the body of the murderer. This resulted in a slow, painful, agonizing death for the condemned.

When we don't release our past offenses, we become the condemned person carrying the toxins and poisons from our past with us. Our past toxins and poisons will eventually destroy us if we hold on to them. You can't overcome your past and hold on to your past at the same time. There has to be a release. Let go of anger, offenses, burdens, sin, failure, unforgiveness, bitterness, toxic relationships, and anything else that is harming you, keeping you defeated, and keeping you from your opportunity of success. Strong Christians are those who have learned to release. The happiest believers are those who have learned to release. The greatest overcomers are those who have learned to release! It is time for you to LET IT GO! That's exactly what God did with your past when he forgave you of your sins. Micah 7:19 says "He will again have compassion on us, and will subdue our iniquities. You will cast all our sins into the depths of the sea."

There comes a time when you must let it go. If not, your past will continually disrupt your life. One day, while Penny and I were dating, we decided to make the 40-mile drive to Gulf Shores, Alabama to walk the beach. It was one of our favorite things to do! The beach is great therapy, and little did I know I was about to get some therapy from Penny! While we were walking and talking through some of my issues from the past there was a piece of paper in the sand, and Penny said pick it up and hold it. As we continued walking there was a drink bottle, and Penny said to pick it up and hold it. Next, there was a drink can, and then a plastic bag. You get the picture. Now I am walking down the beach with both hands filled with trash. And wouldn't you know it, then we saw a toy shovel laying in the sand. Penny said to put down the trash, take that shovel, and dig a hole in the sand. After I dug the hole in the sand she said now put the trash in the hole and cover it up with sand. Once that was done, she said to stand on it, and told me this was a symbolic act of putting all my trash from my past behind me, and it was time to let it go and stop digging it up! It was amazing what that did for me. It was another big step in coming to peace with my past. Bury it, let it go, stop digging it up, and move forward is a powerful lesson I learned on the beach that day from my beautiful Penny!

CHAPTER 12

THE SCARRED LIFE

Comedian Carol Burnett said, "Nobody goes through life without a scar." I agree with her assessment of life one hundred percent. We all have scars. Some people hide their scars better than others can or do. And with some, there is just no hiding it. Scaring is the body's natural way of healing damaged skin. Scars may be formed for many different reasons such as accidents, burns, diseases, injuries, surgeries, or wounds. Scars develop over time as new skin begins to grow over a wound. Visible scars can affect people psychologically. Often people will go to great extents to hide their scars. Life can leave you scared physically, emotionally, mentally, and even spiritually.

The Apostle Paul wrote about scars in Galatians 6:17 "I bear on my body the scars that show I belong to Jesus." Paul had a scarred-up body. He explained how he received his scars in 2 Corinthians 11:24-25. The source of his scars came first from being beaten by Jews 5 times with 39 stripes. Why 39 stripes? The Mosaic Law (Deuteronomy 25:1-3) stated a Judge could sentence a man found guilty of certain crimes to a beating of 40 stripes, but could never go over 40 stripes. The Jews would stop at 39 stripes to make sure they didn't mistakenly violate the law by going over 40. The one administering the beating would be punished if he exceeded the legal number of lashes. The whip used was leather and made of three cords. The guilty man's hands were tied to a post, and his clothes were torn off to his waist leaving his chest and back exposed. He could not stand or sit but had to stoop over to receive 13 stripes to his chest/stomach, 13 stripes to his right shoulder/back, and 13 stripes to his left shoulder/back. This is how a guilty man received 39 strips around his body's torso. Paul suffered this beating 5 times for a total of 195 stripes.

Second, Paul was beaten with rods 3 times. Beaten with rods was a Roman punishment inflicted upon criminals by Roman authorities. The term beaten with rods translates from a Greek verb, rabdizo which is only found twice in the Bible. It means to be beaten with a long, stiff, branch such as a tree limb. The rods were usually made of birch wood. A strong Roman Soldier trained in how to intensely inflict pain would deliver the whipping. There was no limitation of 39 stripes, and the soldier would beat their victims mercilessly all over their bodies. The beatings were so bad that often the victims were beaten to death. Paul experienced this inhumane beating three times.

Next, Paul had been stoned. Stoning was a method of execution in which a group of people would gather around a condemned person and begin casting rocks at the person until death occurred. It was a horrible way to die. Mosaic Law specified that before anyone could be put to death by stoning, there had to be a trial, and at least two witnesses to testify (Deuteronomy 17:6). The two witnesses who testified against the condemned person in court had to cast the first stone. Death by stoning was prescribed in the Old Testament for various sins such as murder, idolatry, occults, blaspheming, and sexual sins.

Stoning was also used in the New Testament in persecuting the early Christians. In Acts 14:19-28 a group of Jews from Antioch and Iconium came to Lystra and won the crowds. Then they attacked Paul by stoning him, then dragged him outside the city, and left him for dead. Paul was the victim of misdirected religious zeal and hatred. To the amazement of his people, Paul survived the stoning. This was a remarkable miracle considering the Jews were quite skilled at killing people with stones.

Finally, Paul speaks of surviving a shipwreck 3 times. Paul made many voyages going from Jerusalem to Tarsus, Antioch, various parts of Asia Minor, and Cyprus. Shipwrecks in those seas were not uncommon. Paul speaks of one occasion being in the deep for a day and night. He survived floating in deep waves for 24 hours in a stormy sea by hanging on to a plank, or a fragment of the ship. Paul lived the scared life receiving five whippings (195 stripes), three beatings with rods, a stoning, and three shipwrecks. Yes, Paul knew something about scars.

God designed the human body to heal itself. If you suffer from a burn, cut, or scrap your body has the amazing ability to recover. While the assistance of antibiotics and medication is often needed that takes nothing away from the natural ability the body has to recover from an accident or illness. Recovery often includes the development of a scar. The healing of a wound includes the forming of a scab which falls off as new skin develops to the creation of a scar which is a process that takes time.

SCARS REMIND YOU OF THE FAITHFULNESS OF GOD

Lamentations 3:22-23 "The unfailing love of The Lord never ends! By his mercies, we have been kept from destruction. Great is his faithfulness; his mercies begin afresh each day." This scripture teaches us that God's faithfulness is unchanging and always available to us. As a senior adult, David writes about God's faithfulness in Psalm 37:25 "Once I was young, and now I am old. Yet I have never seen the godly forsaken, nor seen their children begging for bread." David had seen the good, bad, and ugly in life, but in his last days, the thing that stands out more than anything is God's faithfulness. When you look back and reminisce at life God's faithfulness will stand out more than anything. Scars are a testimony to the faithfulness of God. God didn't keep you from the battle, but he kept you in the battle! He didn't keep you from disappointment, but he kept you while you were in the disappointment! He didn't keep you from failure, but he kept you while you were in failure! The pain, but he kept you while you were in the pain! He didn't keep you from the storm, but he kept you while you were in the storm! He didn't keep you from the trial, but he kept you while you were in the trial! He didn't keep you from the valley, but he kept you while you were passing through the valley!

1 Corinthians 10:13 tells us that "No temptation has overtaken you except what is common to mankind. And God is faithful, he will not let you be tempted beyond what you can

bear. But when you are tempted, he will also provide a way out so that you can endure it."

SCARS KEEP YOU IN CHECK

People who do not learn from past failures repeat them. Repeated failures keep you in bondage. Remember the words of Galatians 5:1, "Stand fast therefore in the liberty wherewith Christ hath made us free, and be not entangled again with the yoke of bondage." Scars have a way of keeping us in check by serving as reminders of our past failures, and poor choices. God can use the scars of our lives to say to us, don't go there again. Ignoring scars means you have not learned from your past failures, and you are setting yourself up for self-inflicted wounds. David was a man with some self-inflicted scars in his life. He brought a lot of pain to himself by some very selfish decisions. While God forgave him of his sin of adultery with Bathsheba (Psalm 51), the scar of his sin followed him to his grave. Proverbs 6:27-35 teaches the sin of adultery leaves a scar that never fades. A person can be forgiven and restored, and still carry the scars of sin. Scars can serve as a reminder of your weaknesses and struggles. Scars can remind you of how vulnerable you can be.

In other words, you can't trust your flesh. In the Bible, the word flesh refers to our old sinful nature, but it can also be about our abilities and capacities. It wasn't God who led David into adultery with Bathsheba. It was his own flesh. Jesus said the flesh is weak (Matthew 26:41), and profits nothing (John 6:63). The Apostle Paul said his flesh produced nothing good (Romans 7:18), and that he had no confidence in the flesh (Philippians 3:3). There is not one scripture in the Bible that compliments the flesh. Scars can give you a reality check by reminding you of how your flesh failed you, and why you need God in your life.

SCARS TELL YOUR STORY

Every scar has a story. It could be from a fishing or hunting accident, a cut on your hand from a knife while cooking, or a surgical incision. I have a scar on my right leg two inches below my knee from a bicycle wreck I had when I was about ten years old. The wreck took place while I was playing at Grandma Susie's house. While I was bleeding and going crazy my grandmother settled me down, cleaned my wound, medicated it, wrapped it with gauze, and of course put a band-aid on it. Back in the day we rarely went to the doctor. Almost all injuries were taken care of at home. In time the wound healed and left a scar. That scar has been on my leg for over fifty years, and when I look at it I still remember my bicycle wreck. It doesn't hurt now, but it does bring back a memory. It tells a story. Often a scar represents something traumatic, and people are reluctant to share their story because of the pain involved.

There could come a day when God opens a door for you to share your story. Sharing your story will be a blessing to someone, and healing for you. Sharing your story doesn't mean you have to give every detail. There may be parts of your story that you always keep to yourself. Revelation 12:11 "They overcame him (Satan) by the blood of the lamb and by the word of their testimony." Their testimony was their story! Also, ALWAYS let your story bring God glory!

SCARS PROVE YOU ARE A SURVIVOR

Surviving isn't always glitz and glamor as seen on television. It isn't always pretty, in fact, it can leave you beaten up, bruised, and worn out. You can survive and not be celebrated. You can survive and not be recognized, or noticed. But you survived! You could have given up, but you didn't. You stood against all odds and you made it. You made it when some people wrote you off, threw you away, or forgot about you. Hold your head up. You're a survivor!

Survivors usually carry scars. Scars are proof you're alive. When Thomas questioned Jesus after the resurrection, Jesus showed him his scars. Scars don't grow on what is dead, but only on what is alive! Scars are a sign of life, not death. In the beginning, a scar can be very sensitive, and you need to protect it. But there will come a day when it is healed. It will no longer be painful. I can look at the scar from my bicycle wreck now and there is no pain whatsoever. A scar is no longer a wound. So don't treat a scar like a wound. You don't have to continually medicate a scar.

Give God praise for surviving. In Psalm 124 David said, If it had not been the Lord who was on our side...the enemy would have swallowed Israel up." David then exhorts Israel to praise God for surviving because Israel didn't survive by itself. God helped them. You didn't survive by yourself. God helped you! If the enemy could have taken you out he would have, but God helped you! You didn't fight the battle by yourself, God helped you! You survived because God helped you!

SCARS TEACH YOU CONTENTMENT

Contentment is defined as an emotional state of satisfaction. It isn't settling for less, but coming to the place of accepting one's situation, and moving forward when your life has had a major setback. One of the Apostle Paul's greatest statements is found in Philippians 4:11 "I have learned to be content whatever the circumstances." Notice Paul didn't say, God made me content, or God just drop all this contentment into my heart. It was a lesson he had to learn. Paul didn't learn contentment from a book, classroom, or instructor. Some of life's greatest lessons come from living life. Contentment is a valuable lesson to learn. Contentment isn't an easy lesson to learn. It can be complicated and at times difficult. It's a lesson you may have to learn more than once. Learning the lesson of contentment will help you grow stronger, and develop as a mature Christian.

How can a person learn contentment? By living according to priorities. Priorities will bring order to your life. Jesus taught order in Matthew 6:33 "Seek the Kingdom of God above all else, and live righteously, and he will give you everything you need." Priorities bring order, and order brings blessings. Priorities reveal what you value, and what is important to you. Your list of priorities should be as follows: God, your spouse, your family, your health, your job, your finances, your friends, and your church.

We also learn contentment when we accept what we can't change. One of the most difficult challenges in life is accepting what you can't change. Beating yourself up, and feeling guilty over something you have no control over will not change anything in your past or present. Alcoholics Anonymous repeats the serenity prayer regularly in their meetings. It states, "God, grant me the serenity to accept the things I cannot change, the courage to change the things I can, and the wisdom to know the difference." This is a powerful prayer that can help anyone who is dealing with situations that seem to be unchangeable.

Contentment comes when we keep the past where it belongs, behind us!

I once heard John Maxwell say, "The past is past because it's past." One of the blessings of being a new creation in Christ is "old things are passed away" (II Corinthians 5:17). Allowing your past to be in the present will rob you of so many moments of joy. Live in the now. Living in the now brings so many rewards. Living in the past will only produce regrets. I love a small phrase in Galatians 2:20 "the life that I now live." These words come from a man (Paul) who had a dreadful past, became a new creation in Christ, and is living in the now with his past behind him.

When you Feed Your Spirit you learn contentment. Your spirit needs a constantly balanced diet of the Word of God. Just as our physical bodies have to be fed to have strength our spirits have to be fed to be strong. After his baptism, Jesus is led by the Holy Spirit to the wilderness. Jesus was in the wilderness for forty days and fasted while he was there (Matthew 4). When Satan comes to Jesus he appears to be physically vulnerable, and Satan tempts him to turn stones into bread. Jesus responds by quoting

Deuteronomy 8:3 "Man does not live on bread alone, but on every word that comes from the mouth of God." Jesus overcome temptation with a weak body and a strong spirit! That's why feeding your spirit is so important. Paul wrote in II Corinthians 4:16, "That is why we never give up. Though our bodies are dying, our spirits are being renewed every day."

When we Press On in the Christian race we grow in contentment. There will be bad days. Sometimes emotions get the best of you. Negative memories can flood your mind. When it all comes back with a force, and you are having panic attacks take a deep breath and put everything on pause. Take a timeout. That's what ball teams do when things are going bad for them during a game. The timeout is for them to gain their composure, make adjustments, and refocus. Then tell yourself, I can handle this! That's right, talk to yourself, and tell yourself you can get through it. Next, connect with a friend who will listen to you, and pray will you. Having a backup and support friend is a great plan. Jesus said in Matthew 18:19 "If two of you on earth agree about anything you ask for, it will be done for you by my Father in heaven." Lastly, believe tomorrow is going to be a better day! Mark 9:23 "Anything is possible if a person believes."

The old saying, Count Your Blessings, really creates contentment. Psalm 103:2 "Bless the Lord. O my soul, and forget not all his benefits." Start and keep a list of God's blessings in your life. Include small blessings, big blessings, everyday blessings, material blessings, financial blessings, personal blessings, and spiritual blessings. Never forget the source of your blessings is

God. James 1:17 reminds us that "Every good and perfect gift is from above, coming down from the Father." Maintain an attitude of gratitude. Do away with the entitlement mentality of believing that one is deserving of privileges or special treatment. Blessings do not come from God based upon who deserves it, but because of his goodness. We have a good, good Heavenly Father! Look for the goodness of God daily and you will see it. The Psalmist wrote in Psalm 68:19, "Blessed be the Lord, who daily loads us with benefits."

Focus On The Future and contentment grows. There is no future in the past. Your tomorrows are not in your yesterdays. Focusing on the future will bring a sense of purpose. Everybody needs a purpose. Everyone needs to feel that their life is significant and that they make a contribution to mankind. No matter how bad or big your setbacks were, you are not done in life.

There is a reason you are still here. You can't stop living. When you stop living you stop giving. The purpose is only fulfilled by people who live their lives giving. The future is important because it offers you new challenges which can lead to new accomplishments in fulfilling your purpose.

Your scars can serve as a reminder that you have been hurt, or that you have been healed. You choose which one it will be. Are you going to live the rest of your life hurt or healed? Make up your mind that you will not live wounded for the rest of your life. Remember, Psalm 147:3 "He heals the brokenhearted binding up their wounds." A scar is much easier to live with if you allow it to remind you that you're a survivor, not a victim. Let your scars be a testimony that speaks of the faithfulness of God, and an encouragement to others that you made it through a difficult time, and they can too.

CHAPTER 13

GOD'S AFFIRMATION

In its best sense, affirmation is a declaration that something is true. It is a statement of endorsement and support. Affirmation is far more than unrealistic wishful thinking, and empty words. When affirming a person you are embracing an individual's values, character, and goals. The power of affirmation is seen in how it can improve self-esteem, raise confidence, and boost motivation. It can bring significant changes to one's state of mind that enables a person to overcome doubts, criticism, and negativity. The simple words, "I believe in you," can provide the inspiration an insecure person may need to accept a challenge before them or finish a task that needs to be completed.

The church at Corinth was far from perfect. In his two letters to the believers in Corinth the Apostle Paul had to deal with many issues, and wrote many words of instruction and correction. Yet, with all the church's problems and conflict Paul also gave them great words of confirmation in II Corinthians 1:21-22. I love the following two translations of this scripture. The first is from the New International Version and the second one is from The Message.

"Now it is God who makes both us and you stand firm in Christ. He anointed us, set his seal of ownership on us, and put his Spirit in our hearts as a deposit, guaranteeing what is to come."

"God affirms us, making us a sure thing in Christ, putting His Yes within us. By his Spirit, he has stamped us with his eternal pledge-a sure beginning of what he is destined to complete."

Children have many needs while going through the infant, toddler, childhood, and adolescence stages of becoming an adult. The two greatest needs of children from parents are affirmation and correction. Affirmation occurs when a child hears their parents say, "I love you," " I'm proud of you," and "You can do it." An affirmation can come from words, hugs, kisses, gifts, and involvement in school projects and events. Dad and mom spending time with children are affirming.

Correction is equally important. When a parent sees behavior in a child that is not good the parent has a responsibility to give correction to the child. No child should ever be abused, but every child needs discipline. You correct the child because you love the child, and know if you don't give correction now the behavior will only get worse later. Proverbs 13:24 "Whoever spares the rod hates their children, but the one who loves their children is careful to discipline them."

Isn't it amazing that even as adults we never grow out of these two needs? We still need affirmation and correction as we mature. The same needs, but a different form of affirmation, and a different kind of correction. When Jesus came to earth he came full of grace and truth (John 1:14). Jesus brought to earth our two greatest needs. First, he brought grace. Grace affirms. Paul stated in I Corinthians 15:10 "By the grace of God I am what I am." Second, he brought the truth. Truth corrects. Hebrews 12:6 "Whom The Lord loves he corrects." Our two greatest needs in life are found in Christ.

God works by affirmation. God affirms us as His children by His Word and by His Spirit.

HIS WORD

Romans 10:9-10 "For if you confess with your mouth that Jesus is Lord and believe in your heart that God raised him from the dead, you will be saved. For it is by believing in your heart that you are made right with God, and it is by confessing with your mouth that you are saved."

HIS SPIRIT

Romans 8:14-16 "For all who are led by the Spirit of God are the children of God. So you should not be like cowering, fearful slaves. You should behave instead like God's very own children, adopted into his family--calling him Father, dear Father. For his Holy Spirit speaks to us deep in our hearts and tells us that we are God's children.

Satan works by accusation. Revelation 12:11 identifies Satan as the Accuser of the brethren, accusing them before God day and night. In Job chapter one Satan comes before God and has a conversation with God about Job. In the conversation, God affirms Job (verse 8) declaring him to be the greatest man on all the earth. A man of character and integrity. Then Satan accuses Job (verses 9-11) of only serving God for what he can get out of God insisting that if God took everything away from Job, he would curse God.

God works through affirmation building people up while Satan works through accusation tearing people down. God's Word and Spirit affirm us as his children.

Knowing who you are, and whose you are can be the difference between victory and defeat. Martin Luther, who sparked the Protestant Reformation, said, "The Holy Spirit is no skeptic. He has written neither doubt nor mere opinion into our hearts, but rather solid assurances, which are more sure and solid than all experience and even life itself."

The baptism of Jesus by John the Baptist in the River Jordan is recorded in all four gospels. John feels unqualified to baptize Jesus and he tries to get out of it by stating he wasn't worthy to untie your sandals. Jesus persists and the baptism takes place. During the baptism the heavens opened, the Holy Spirit descends as a dove landing on Jesus' shoulder, and the Father said, "This is my beloved Son in whom I'm well pleased." While Jesus was being baptized the Father affirmed him. This is far more than a religious ceremony, it is an affirmation of Jesus. Everyone there knows Jesus was the Son of God. Remember, God affirms us by his Word and by his Spirit. In the river the Father affirmed Jesus by his Word, saying this is my Son, and by his Spirit descending as a dove.

Immediately after his baptism, Jesus is led by the Holy Spirit to the wilderness where he fasted for forty days (Matthew 4:1-11). The wilderness is a dry, hot, barren, and lonely place. Jesus is fasting and spending time alone preparing for his public ministry to begin. It is here that Satan comes to Jesus saying, "If you're the son of God" (verses 3, 5) and "If you will bow down and worship me" (verse 9). Three times Satan uses the word if with a challenge connected to it. He is trying to get Jesus to doubt who he is. Doubt can be sowed in very small seeds. The word if only has two letters in it, but is very destructive because of the doubt it produces. The enemy will use little seeds of doubt to get you to second-guess yourself, and every decision you've made. Doubt has never answered a prayer, moved a mountain, provided a solution, brought healing to someone, or encouraged anyone,

In the river the Father affirmed Jesus. In the wilderness Satan doubted Jesus. It is when you're going through dry, hard, hot, barren, and lonely times that Satan loves to start sowing seeds of doubt in your life. I love Jesus' response. Every time Satan used the word if against him Jesus began quoting scripture, It is written..... When the enemy tries to get you to question who you are in Christ, or your purpose, go to the Word of God for affirmation.

The Father's affirmation would be with Jesus throughout his earthly ministry. The Father knew the opposition Jesus would encounter and affirmed him in advance. Look at what Jesus encountered during his ministry:

- Satan tempted him (Matthew 4:3-10),

- The Jews rejected him (John 1:11),
- The World hated him (John 15:25),
- The Nazarenes dishonored him (Matthew 13:53-58),
- The Sadducees opposed him (Matthew 22:23-32),
- The Pharisees accused him of working by the power of Satan (Matthew 12:24) and challenged his authority. (Matthew 12:38-42), faulted him for eating with sinners. (Mark 2:16), called him a drunk. (Luke 7:34), declared him to be a false prophet. (7:39) criticized him for healing on the Sabbath. (Luke 13:10-17), threatened to stone him. (John 10:31), claimed he was a blasphemer. (John 10:33), conspired to kill him. (John 11:47-53),
- John the Baptist questioned him (Luke 7:18-23),
- Judas betrayed him (Matthew 26:14-16),
- Peter denied him (Luke 22:57-60),
- The Chief Priest charged him with many crimes (Mark 15:3),
- The crowd on Friday turned on him (Matthew 27:22),
- The Roman soldiers crucified him (Matthew 27:32-44),
- After the resurrection Thomas doubted him (John 20:24-25),

None of this changed who Jesus was because the Father had affirmed him in the river. None of this stopped Jesus from fulfilling his purpose because the Father had affirmed him. After all the rejection, hatred, opposition, criticism, doubting, and betrayal Jesus was still the Son of God. Once the Father has affirmed you, and your purpose in life no amount of opposition can ever change it.

II Corinthians 1:21-22 is all about affirmation. It is a God saying, I believe in you. You don't have to be perfect for God to affirm you. God doesn't use perfect people to build his Kingdom because there aren't any perfect people. God uses people with weaknesses, limitations, baggage, hangups, and faults. His affirmation can make up the difference.

In the Bible, we find that God affirmed many people whom we remember for their exploits and miracles.

- Abraham with Isaac after Abraham had fathered Ishmael,
- Joseph after his brothers had rejected him, and sold him into slavery,
- Moses led Israel after he had offered all his excuses at the burning bush,
- David to be King of Israel when he was a shepherd boy at the age of 15,
- Elijah after he hides from Jezebel under a tree so depressed he wants to die,
- Job after he had questioned God with twice as much as he originally had,
- Peter after he denied Christ three times but became a pillar of the church,
- Paul who hated Christianity declared him to be a chosen vessel,

Let's take a closer look at II Corinthians 1:21-22 and find how God affirms his people.

HE STRENGTHENS US

(Verse 21) He makes us stand firm in Christ. He supplies us with the strength to stand when the pressure is on. When the weight of the moment seems too heavy he gives us the ability to stand. In Ephesians chapter six Paul gives us instructions about putting on the whole armor of God. Every good soldier knows the importance of each piece of the armor, and how to wear it. Without the armor, a soldier doesn't have much of a chance of defeating the enemy. The soldier's armor is a major key to his success. Then Paul gives us another key to a soldier's success by using the word stand.

Four times he uses the word stand in Ephesians chapter 6. Look at verse 11 - "Put on the whole armor of God so that you will be able to stand against strategies and tricks of the devil."

Verse 13 - Use every piece of God's armor to stand against the enemy in the time of evil.

Verse 13 - So that after the battle you will be standing firm.

Verse 14 - Stand your ground, putting on the belt of truth, and breastplate or body armor of righteousness.

Paul doesn't say to put on the Armor of God and run or hide. He said stand. Often your greatest victories come from standing. Standing may not look very spiritual to some people because they base spirituality on excitement, enthusiasm, movement, or volume. Yet, there are times when the best thing you can do is hold on to your promise from God and stand. God will give you the strength to stand.

HE SANCTIFIES US

The word sanctify means to be set apart. This is the whole concept Paul is trying to reveal in 2 Corinthians 6:16-17 when he stated believers are the Temple of The Lord, and should not be involved in idol worship. Then in verse 17, he declared, Christians should come out from them, and be separate. It is important to note that sanctification is based on separation, not isolation. There is a big difference between separation and isolation. Cults often operate by isolation. They live to themselves, by themselves, and for themselves. Jesus never taught isolation. You can't isolate yourself from the world and change the world. Matthew 5:13-16 taught that Christians are the salt of the earth and the light of the world. In John 17:15-21 Jesus taught believers are in the world, but not of the world. In Mark 16:15 some of Jesus' last words to his disciples were, "Go into all the world and preach the Good News to everyone, everywhere."

When God affirms us he sets us apart for his purpose. He has a design in mind. He has a reason for the separation. Just like when God called Paul a chosen vessel or instrument in Acts 9:15 and separated him first in Damascus before anointing him for his purpose of preaching Jesus. The act of sanctifying (separation), and the work of anointing always go together. God separates and then anoints. Jeremiah wrote about God separating him before he was even born in Jeremiah 1:5 (NLT) "I knew you before I formed you in your mother's womb. Before you were born I set you apart and appointed you as my spokesman to the world."

HE ANOINTS US

In the Old Testament, there were three callings for men to serve: the Prophet, the Priest, and the King. Once a person was sanctified and anointed they were authorized to serve in their calling. A Prophet was anointed to speak the Word of the Lord to people. A Priest was anointed to pray for people, and a King was anointed to lead people. The three greatest spiritual needs of people are 1. To hear the word of the Lord. Romans 10:17 "Faith comes by hearing, and hearing by the word of God." 2. To petition the Lord. Matthew 6:11 "Give us this day our daily bread."3. To be directed by the Lord. Jesus referred to us as sheep. One of the tendencies of sheep is to wander. Isaiah 53:6 "All we like sheep have gone astray." God calls, sanctifies, and anoints people to minister to the three greatest spiritual needs of people. God always anoints a person for someone else. The anointing is not to make someone look good or sound good, but to minister to the needs of people.

HE SEALS US

Verse 22 describes that He sets his seal of ownership on us. Ancient seals were made of wax embedded with the personalized imprint of a King's ring. A King would declare a decree by taking his signet ring and stamping it into warm wax. Anytime official transactions took place the King's ring would be used to authorize and seal legal documents. Sealed documentations were completely the possession of the King. The seal meant ownership.

In affirming us as his children our Heavenly Father has full ownership. Our seal is the cross because it was on the cross that God's son, Jesus, conquered sin, and redeemed us. The word redeemed means to gain or regain possession of something in exchange for payment. Jesus crucified was payment for our sinful debt. The exchange was our freedom from sin. Paul describes this powerful exchange in Colossians 2:14-15 "Having canceled the charge of our legal indebtedness, which stood against us and condemned us, he has taken it away, nailing it to the cross. And having disarmed the powers and authorities, he made a public spectacle of them, triumphing over them by the cross."

When we believe that Christ died for our sins, and confess his lordship (Romans 10:10) the exchange is applied to our lives and we are sealed by the Holy Spirit. Ephesians 1:13-14 says "When you believed, you were marked in him with a seal, the promised Holy Spirit, who is a deposit guaranteeing our inheritance until the redemption of those who are God's possession."

Once again, a seal represents ownership which brings security. We are secure in Christ according to Colossians 1:14 "In whom we have redemption, the forgiveness of sins." We have been redeemed from our sins by Christ's death on the cross, and our salvation is sealed by the Holy Spirit. We find the word, seal, again in Ephesians 4:30, "Do not grieve the Holy Spirit of God, with whom you were sealed for the day of redemption."

The Holy Spirit was involved in creation (Genesis 1:2), the virgin birth of Jesus (Luke 1:34-35), the baptism of Jesus (Luke 3:21-22), the ministry of Jesus (Acts 10:38), the resurrection of Jesus (Romans 8:11), birth of the church (Acts 2), and the writing of scripture (2 Peter 1:19-21). The same Holy Spirit is involved in our salvation as Jesus explained to Nicodemus in John 3:1-8.

HE SEES OUR FUTURE

Again in verse 22, He put the Holy Spirit in our hearts as a deposit guaranteeing what is to come. Often in financial transactions such as purchasing a house or car a down payment is required. It may be a 10% or 20% deposit. The deposit is a part of the process of making a purchase. It is a part of the investment you are making. It reserves your purchase for now and begins the financing for the future. God always works with the future in mind. He sees beyond the now into the tomorrow. The Lord spoke through the Prophet Jeremiah to Israel while they were in Babylon captivity these powerful words in Jeremiah 29:11 "For I know the plans I have for you, declares the Lord, plans to prosper you and not to harm you, plans to give you hope and a future." While Israel had been in Babylon captivity for seventy years God was reassuring them of their future. Look at what God also told Israel in Jeremiah 29:14 "I will end your captivity, and restore your fortunes." God saw their future, and their future looked nothing like their present. God sees your future now, and your future looks much brighter than your present. Everything God has done for you is just a deposit for what is to come in your future. God knows where you are now, and has planned your future. No matter how bad the past was, or present is, with God, you always have hope and a future. Your best days are not behind you, your best days are ahead of you. You can hold on to Jeremiah 29:11 & 14, and declare my best is to come!

A beautiful scene of affirmation takes place in the story of the prodigal son in Luke 15:11-32. As the story unfolds, it reveals the unique relationship between the son and his father, first parting and then returning.

THE STORY BEGINS WITH THE SON

- Demanding his inheritance from his father,
- Leaving for a distant country,
- Wasting all the money his father had given him on wild living,
- Experiencing the hardships of a famine that came unexpectedly,
- Getting a job on a farm feeding pigs,
- Finally coming to his senses and realizes how good he had it at home,
- Declaring he would return home,
- Confessing to his father he was unworthy of a son, and
- Asking his father if he could just be a hired hand on his estate,

THE STORY CONTINUES WITH THE FATHER

- Seeing his son coming from a great distance,
- Running to embrace and kiss his returning son,
- Instructing his staff to bring the best robe and put it on his son, get a ring for his finger, and sandals for his feet,
- Throwing a welcome home party for his son,
- Declaring "My son was lost, but now is found! My son was dead, but now is alive!",
- Defending his wayward son to the older brother, and

- Assuring the older son, "Everything I have is yours."

What a picture of affirmation! The father embraced and kissed his son. Then he gave him a robe, a ring, and sandals. Next, the father called for a party so they could celebrate his son's return home. When the son was at his worst, the father was at his best! When the son was wrong the father never stopped loving him. When the son was eaten up with guilt and feeling unworthy, the father accepted him. When the son requested to be a servant, the father would only address him as "my son." The father never changed the son's status. The son left home as a son and returned as a son.

This powerful picture of affirmation represents how our Heavenly Father responds to us when we come to him in such an unworthy condition. No one who has ever come to God received condemnation or judgment. Everyone who comes to God receives love, acceptance, forgiveness, and affirmation. This is how Jesus dealt with the woman at the well, with Zacchaeus in the sycamore tree, and the thief on the cross. This is how Jesus will deal with you because He loves you, accepts you, forgives you, and affirms you.

CHAPTER 14

EXTREME MAKEOVER

Extreme Makeover was an American reality television program that aired for ten seasons (2003-2012). It premiered on ABC on December 11, 2002, and was hosted by Ty Pennington. The program's objective was to locate a deserving family whose home needed renovation. Extreme Makeover would sponsor the family for a week's vacation, and work 24/7 to complete their home's makeover. The design team had crews of carpenters, electricians, plumbers, painters, and roofers lined up to tackle every project involved in the home improvements inside and outside. Once the renovations were completed new home furnishings were placed throughout the house. Even landscaping was a part of the renovation. It was amazing to see what the design team accomplished in one week. The highlight of the show was watching the expressions and responses of family members viewing their home for the first time after the makeover.

Long before people were making extreme makeovers with houses, buildings, cars, or furniture God was performing extreme makeovers with people. We find it in Jeremiah 18:4 "So he made it again into another vessel." God spoke to Jeremiah to go down to the Potter's house. God speaking to people was nothing new. He spoke to Adam, Noah, Abraham, Moses, Joshua, and many more. However, when God spoke to Jeremiah he instructed him to go to the Potter's house (Jeremiah 18:1-4), and from there Jeremiah would receive the revelation God had for him. In other words, God was going to use a potter working with clay as a visual aid for Jeremiah.

From that image, Jeremiah would learn some valuable lessons concerning God's relationship with his people. Teachers know the power of visual aids, and how students learn much more from what they see than from what they hear.

The analogy of a Potter working with clay is also found in Isaiah 64:8 and Romans 9:21. In these scriptures we see the creativity of the potter taking the lowly substance of clay, and making different types of vessels. The Potter is in full control molding clay into a jar, plate, pot, or bowl that is needed, and useful. This is the whole concept of Ephesians 2:10 "For we are God's masterpiece. He has created us anew in Christ Jesus so that we can do the good things he planned for us long ago."

The Potter began working with clay by adding water. Water brings clay to life. Clay particles won't cohere without water, and if they won't stick together, the potter can't shape them. Water is a necessary component in pottery. It has to be involved in the process from the beginning. Water represents the Holy Spirit. The Holy Spirit is essential to life. On the last day of the Festival of Tabernacles (John 7:37-39) Jesus stood and shouted, "If you're thirsty, come to me. If you believe in me, come and drink! For the scriptures declare that rivers of living water will flow out from within." Verse 39 tells us when Jesus spoke of living water he was speaking of the Spirit.

Next, the Potter would start kneading the clay. Kneading meant working the clay into a uniform mixture by pressing, folding, and stretching it with one's hands. During the Kneading process, the Potter would become aware of stones or other objects mixed in with the clay, and remove them.

After the Kneading was completed the clay was placed on the center of the wheel. The wheel was made of stone and represents the continual revolving circumstances of life. The Potter would petal the wheel with his feet, and shape the clay with his hands as he held it on the center of the wheel. With the motion of the wheel, the potter molded the clay into the vessel he desired.

Not all clay vessels go into Potter's desired shape the first time on the wheel. If the clay isn't forming as the Potter desires it is taken off the wheel and put back in the mill. Then the process starts all over again.

When observing a Potter working with clay what did Jeremiah discover? What was the lesson God could teach him from pottery? While watching the daily routine of pottery being developed what could Jeremiah have learned? How could a Potter's hands working with a wheel speak to Jeremiah? Let's examine Jeremiah 18:4 to see what God is trying to teach Jeremiah from pottery.

THE PROBLEM WITH THE CLAY

Verse 4 "The vessel that he made of clay was marred." The word marred means that the clay had defects, imperfections, and flaws. Marred clay represents humanity. It represents everyone. Romans 3:23 "For all have sinned and fall short of the glory of God." Sin is a part of the human race's DNA because of the fall of the first man, Adam. The good news is Christ has redeemed us from sin by his death on the cross. Yet, we have to keep in mind that salvation is redemption, not perfection. Christians are not perfect, just forgiven. This is not an excuse for not doing your best to live a life pleasing to God. However, the truth is even our best is not perfect. You will never know perfection until you are in heaven. God uses people with problems, shortcomings, and faults to build his Kingdom.

Here is a list of some imperfect people God used for his cause or purpose in the Bible:

- Noah had a drinking problem.
- Abraham slept with Hagar and fathered Ishmael.
- Moses had anger issues and murdered an Egyptian.
- Jacob was a liar and a deceiver.
- Elijah battled depression and was suicidal.
- David was an adulterer and a murderer.
- Solomon was a sex addict with 1,000 partners.
- Samson was a womanizer.
- Jonah was hard-headed, and wouldn't listen.

- John the Baptist baptized Jesus and later questioned who he was.
- Peter walked on water with Jesus and later denied him.
- Thomas saw Jesus perform miracles and later doubted him.
- Paul persecuted Christians and confessed to being the worst of sinners.

Even the greatest in God's Kingdom has weaknesses. It goes with humanity. We are all marred. We all need God's grace, love, and forgiveness. Don't use your weakness as an excuse not to serve the Lord. God can help you with your weaknesses, and you may be amazed at how the Lord can use you for his Kingdom. When we give our weaknesses to God he uses them for his glory, and we become stronger where we were once weak.

THE PATIENCE OF THE POTTER.

Verse 4 (NKJV) "So he made it again."Upon discovering the clay's imperfections the potter chose to place the clay back on the wheel and start over with it. Understand the potter has options. He could have said, I don't have time to start over with this clay and thrown it away. He could have said, the imperfections are just too bad for me to work with and thrown it away. He could have said, this clay has lost its value, it won't amount to anything, and thrown it away. But the potter chooses to start all over with defective clay. His patience is on display as much as anything at the Potter's house. David describes God's patience in Psalm 86:15 "But you, Lord, are a compassionate and gracious God, slow to anger, abounding in love and faithfulness."

We see the patience of Jesus in dealing with Simon Peter. The night before Christ's crucifixion Peter denies him 3 times. The pressure of the moment overwhelmed him, and he falls apart denying Jesus. Later, after the resurrection Jesus meets up with Peter one morning (John 21). Jesus doesn't throw Peter away because of his denial, but reaffirms him by asking him three times,

"Do you love me?" Notice the question is not, how could you have denied me after all I've done for you? The simple question is, do you love me? was the beginning of Peter's restoration. If you can answer that question in the affirmative there is hope for you no matter what is in your past. After Peter answers Jesus' question three times by saying, "Yes Lord I love you," Jesus reinstates Peter to ministry by saying, "Feed my sheep" three times. The repeated questioning by Jesus was intentional. This was not just a casual conversation between two friends. This was not just Jesus walking Peter through a painful conversation after a great failure. It was Jesus taking the time to restore Peter and prepare him for the future. A future in which Peter would be a key leader. On that morning Jesus displayed great patience to a wounded brother by restoring from his failure and preparing him for his future role in the Kingdom

THE PROCESS CONTINUES

Verse 4, "Into another vessel, as it seemed good to the potter to make."

The potter continues working with marred clay and develops it into another vessel. The design of the new vessel came from the mind of the potter. The potter placed flawed clay back on the wheel and completely redesigned it. Upon completion, the new vessel looked nothing like the old vessel. The results of the new vessel reveal the passion the potter has in never giving up on marred clay. This process of redesigning can be time-consuming, and messy. We see this when there is renovation of a commercial building, a residential home, or a highway project. It will take time, and there will be a mess. Construction zones are very messy. If your life seems like one continuous mess it may be that the potter is still working on you! Don't get discouraged when you're going through the process of God redesigning you with the messy details. Don't let messy details distract you, and drain you of all your energy. Keep your focus on the big picture.

Architects and contractors keep their attention on the project knowing one day the mess will be cleaned up. One day you will be the finished product, and the messy details won't matter.

God never gives up on us and never stops working on us even if he has to redesign us. Hebrews 12:2 describes Jesus as the author and finisher of our faith. We know what Jesus starts he finishes. He will not leave you incomplete or unfinished. Paul reassures us of this in Philippians 1:6 "Being confident of this very thing, that He who has begun a good work in you will complete it until the day of Jesus Christ."

God working in you makes you a construction zone. Living your life under construction means God has not given up on you. Even with all your flaws and mistakes, God has never thrown you away. He simply puts you back on the wheel again and continues designing and perfecting you for his glory. It takes time and can be messy, but trust his process. God can do amazing things with marred clay!

CHAPTER 15

NEVER QUIT!

Winston Churchill served as British Prime Minister during World War Two. He was relentless in his determination and strategies to defeat Germany and Adolfo Hitler. So much so the Russians gave him the nickname, "British Bulldog." After one of the darker periods of the war, Churchill visited his alma mater, Harrow School, which was just outside Central London. Harrow was a military boarding school Churchill entered at age 14 and was a student there from 1888 to 1893. On October 29, 1941, Churchill gave a twenty-minute speech to the students of Harrow School, and delivered one of his most famous statements:

"Never give in, never, never, never, never in nothing, great or small, large or petty. Never give in except to convictions of honor and good sense. Never yield to force, never yield to the apparently might of the enemy."

Churchill knew winning always requires determination. Dedication, discipline, and determination are the recipe for success. When teaching his disciples about enduring hard times in Luke 21 Jesus gave them the key to victory in verse 21 "In your patience possess ye your souls." I also like the New International Version, "Stand firm, and you win life." Everyone possesses gifts and talents, but natural abilities will only take you so far. Many times in life the difference between winning and losing is determination.

Here is Abraham Lincoln's resume: In 1832 defeated for Illinois State Legislature. 1833 failed in business. 1834 elected to Illinois State Legislature. 1835 sweetheart (Ann Rutledge) died. 1836 suffered a nervous breakdown. 1838 defeated for Speaker of Illinois State Legislature. 1843 defeated for nomination for Congress. 1846 elected to Congress. 1849 rejected for a federal position, General Land Officer. 1854 defeated for Senate. 1856 defeated for nomination for Vice-President. 1858 defeated for Senate. 1860 elected President of the United States.

As an Inventor, Thomas Edison made 1,000 unsuccessful attempts at inventing the light bulb. When a reporter asked, How did it feel to fail 1,000 times? Edison replied I didn't fail 1,000 times. The light bulb was an invention with 1,000 steps.

The greatest basketball player in the history of the game, Michael Jordan, said, "I've missed more than 9,000 shots in my career. I've lost almost 300 games. Twenty-six times, I've been trusted to take the game-winning shot and missed. I've failed over and over and over again in my life. And that is why I succeed."

Baseball player, Babe Ruth, hit 714 home runs and struck out 1,330 times in his career.

Henry Ford, the founder of the Ford Motor Company, failed and went broke five times before he succeeded.

Walt Disney was fired by a newspaper editor because he lacked imagination and had no good ideas.

In 1954 Jimmy Denny, manager of the Grand Ole Opry, fired Elvis Presley after one performance. He told Presley, "You ain't going nowhere, son. You ought to go back to drivin' a truck."

The great football coach, Vince Lombardi, said, "It's not whether you get knocked down; it's whether you get back up."

Solomon, the man God blessed with incredible wisdom wrote in Proverbs 24:16 "Though the righteous fall seven times, they rise again." Jesus declared in Matthew 24:14 (NLT) "Those who endure to the end will be saved."

The Bible instructs and exhorts Christians to endure when difficulties come in life. Let's look at three examples of endurance the Scripture gives us.

THE ATHLETE

Hebrews 12:1-2 "Let us strip off every weight that slows us down, especially the sin that so easily hinders our progress. And let us run with endurance the race that God has set before us. We do this by keeping our eyes on Jesus, on whom our faith depends from start to finish."

A good athlete knows that to win, you must eliminate. Athletes never wear heavy clothing or other items that would slow them down or wear them out physically. They are taught to do away with hindrances from performing at their best. An athlete reserving their energy to compete at a high level is a top priority. Eliminating anything that would keep one from finishing strong is a great lesson learned.

A successful athlete also knows you have to endure. There are times when athletes have to push beyond their limits and fight through their pain, even when they feel like their athletic abilities can't take them any further. Physical talents are captivating! However, endurance often makes the difference between winning and losing. Easy victories are not as rewarding as those that test the limits of our endurance.

Another necessity for an athlete is focus. Great athletes understand what it means to focus. An athlete has to keep their head in the game. They cannot allow distractions or mistakes to throw them off balance. Focus requires discipline. Discipline is the necessary ingredient an athlete needs if they are to perform their personal best.

THE SOLDIER

2 Timothy 2:3 "You must endure hardship as a good soldier of Jesus Christ. No one engaged in warfare entangles himself with the affairs of this life, that he may please him who enlisted him as a soldier."

The Apostle Paul had left Timothy in Ephesus to oversee the church there. Paul wrote two letters to the young Pastor Timothy, a protege of Paul. The first letter came when the church was growing and prospering. The theme of Paul's first letter is organization. For the church to operate efficiently from day to day, Paul instructed Timothy to ordain bishops, deacons, and elders.

Paul's second letter to Timothy came when the church was experiencing great persecution and opposition. The theme of Paul's second letter is determination. He uses the example of a soldier to teach Timothy about enduring hard times. If there was anyone who knew about getting through difficult times, it was a soldier. Soldiers had to know how to handle opposition, confront the enemy, and fight to win. This is the fortitude Paul is trying to develop in Timothy. Paul knew seasons change in life. You can go from prospering to persecution quickly. In times of prosperity, Timothy needed to know about the organization, but in persecution, he needed to know about determination.

THE FARMER

James 5:7-8 teaches that "The farmer waits for the precious produce of the soil, being patient about it, until it gets the early and later rains. You too be patient; strengthen your hearts, for the coming of The Lord is near."

The labors of a farmer were never-ending. From sunrise to sunset. Plowing the field with a mule. There were no John Deere tractors. Preparing the field to sow seed. Working the field after the sowing of seed. Harvesting the crops. All of this while never knowing the next day's weather conditions. Not enough rain meant crops would die from the heat of the sun. Too much rain and crops could be destroyed by flooding. No matter the weather conditions, a farmer knew he had to work the field. It was his livelihood. It was his future. The farmer knew that he might experience an unsuccessful year. In that case, he had to prepare for the next year with hopes that it would be better. Farmers knew all about hard labor, hard times, and what it took to survive. It took endurance.

The common denominator for the athlete, soldier, and farmer was determination. Each would encounter hard work, trying times, setbacks, pressure, disappointments, and injuries. Yet, they could endure hardship to experience success.

We see endurance in the life of David. After David brought down Goliath, King Saul turned on him. King Saul was an insecure man. King Saul became angry when the Israelites honored David for defeating the giant Goliath. In an attempt to kill David, King Saul threw his javelin (spear) at David. To save himself, David became a fugitive. He hid in caves, but King Saul was unable to catch him. King Saul, with his army, had the advantage. However, David was a brilliant strategist. As a young man, he had killed a lion, a bear, and a giant. In Psalm 18:34, David spoke of the favor of God as the secret of his warrior spirit, "He trains my hands for battle, my arms can bend a bow of bronze."

David knew he couldn't live on the run forever, so he went to Achish, King of the Philistines, and asked for grace. King Achish gave David and six hundred men who accompanied him, to a place to reside called Ziklag. After settling in at Ziklag, David and his men went back to Achish and asked to join his military. The Philistines' military leaders advised Achish against David's request, stating he could not be trusted. They reminded him that it was David who took down Goliath. Achish sent David and his men back to Ziklag. Upon returning to Ziklag David and his men found it burned to the ground, and their wives and children had been kidnapped by the Amalekites.

David and his 600 mighty men wept until they had no more strength. Out of desperation and grief, David's men talked about stoning him. King Saul was trying to kill David. King Achish had trust issues with David. David's men turned on him and discussed stoning him. David's response is found in 1 Samuel 30:6 "David was greatly distressed because the men were talking of stoning him; each one was bitter in spirit because of his sons and daughters. But David found strength in The Lord his God." The King James Version states, 'David encouraged himself in The Lord his God.'" David didn't quit. David asked God what he should do, and The Lord told him to pursue the Amalekites. They did as the Lord had instructed, and they recovered their wives and children.

What if David had given up at Ziklag? What if David had not encouraged himself in The Lord? What if David had not inquired of The Lord and pursued the Amalekites?

David and his men would have never recovered their wives and children, but it doesn't stop there. In the very next chapter (1 Samuel 31) King Saul was wounded in battle with the Philistines and ended up committing suicide.

II Samuel chapter two records that David became King of the Tribe of Judah. In II Samuel 5, David became King of the nation of Israel. If David had given up when he faced the pressure of loss at Ziklag, he would have never recovered his wife and children, and he would have never ascended to the throne of King of Israel. David's experience reminds us that quitting forfeits destiny.

The greatest testimony a person can have is to be able to say, I didn't quit. While sitting in a Roman prison cell and facing execution the Apostle Paul left Timothy with this great testimony, "I fought hard, finished my race, and never quit" (1 Timothy 4:7). With all the difficulties Paul had encountered in his ministry (Acts 20, 2 Corinthians 11) there were times he could have easily quit, but he didn't. And because Paul never quit he also wrote about the reward that awaited him in heaven (1 Timothy 4:8). As Coach Vince Lombardi said, "Winners never quit, and quitters never win." It's hard to stop a person who just won't quit. Take the advice of Heisman Trophy winner Tim Tebow, "Take a breath. Don't give up. If you quit you will never know what tomorrow held. You will never know what the breakthrough was going to be. You don't know the doors that are just about to open for you."

Take the word "quit" out of your vocabulary. Make up your mind that quitting is not an option. No matter what you've encountered or experienced, quitting is not who you are.

If you've been abandoned, press on.

If you've been abused, press on.

If you've been betrayed, press on.

If you've been deceived, press on.

If you've been disappointed, press on.

If you've been disrespected, press on.

If you've been forgotten, press on.

If you've been hurt, press on.

If you've been misunderstood, press on

If you've been misrepresented, press on.

If you've been offended, press on.

If you've been rejected, press on.

If you've been treated unfairly, press on

If you've been used, press on.

If you've been violated, press on.

If you've been wounded, press on.

NEVER QUIT!

If you're alone, press on.

If you're discouraged, press on.

If you're weak, press on.

If you're struggling, press on.

If you're wondering where God is, press on.

If you're asking, why it happened, press on

If your dream has been destroyed, press on.

If your past is used against you, press on.

If you have lost friends, press on.

If you feel like a failure, press on.

If you feel like you have nothing to live for, press on.

If you feel like giving up, press on.

If you think you're too damaged, press on.

If you think things are too bad, press on.

If you think you have too much baggage, press on.

If you think the pain is never going to end, press on.

If you think it's too late, press on.

If you are fearful of trying again, press on.

If you can't see any future, press on.

If all the odds are against you, press on.

If all your options are gone, press on.

If it means starting all over again, press on.

Regardless of what life-altering event has come your way, how bad the fallout was, or how painful the loss you encountered, press on. You're not a quitter! You are worth the fight. You deserve to win. You will look back one day and say, I'm so glad I didn't give up. Overcoming is all about making the decision not to quit, and having determination to try again. God is for you (Romans 8:32), and is working everything for your good (Romans 8:28). Don't forfeit what God has for you by quitting. Don't give up on the future God is working out for you by quitting. Don't miss your beauty for ashes by quitting. You are not a quitter. You are a conqueror! Quitters never conquer, and Conquerors never quit. You didn't start this race to quit it. You started this race to finish it. PRESS ON, REGARDLESS!

"Forgetting the past and looking forward to what lies ahead,

I press on to reach the end of the race

and receive the heavenly

prize for which God,

Through Christ Jesus,

is calling us."

Philippians 3:13-14

ABOUT THE AUTHOR

Gary Taylor is a name synonymous with a lifetime of unwavering dedication to full-time ministry. A graduate of Lee University in 1981, his journey has been a testament to his profound commitment to serving the Lord.

With 24 years of experience as a Lead Pastor and an additional 18 years as an International Evangelist, Gary's ministry has left an indelible mark on countless lives. His powerful messages have resonated within local churches, Campmeetings, Conferences, and even on television, showcasing his versatility as a communicator of God's Word.

Gary's reach extends far beyond the United States, as he has brought his inspiring message to 27 of the 50 states and to other nations such as Haiti, Honduras, India, and Israel. He is renowned for his unique ability to minister with the heart of a Pastor, providing spiritual guidance, and the passion of an Evangelist, igniting the flames of faith.

In his debut book, "Press On Regardless," Gary Taylor brings his wealth of ministry experience and deep faith to offer a message of hope and healing. It's a reflection of his life's work, reminding readers that, with God's guidance, they too can press on, regardless of life's challenges, finding the path to wholeness and a brighter future in Christ. Gary Taylor's ministry is a testament to a life devoted to sharing God's love and restoration.

GaryTaylorMinistries@gmail.com

Made in the USA
Columbia, SC
02 June 2025